ASSESSING SECOND LANGUAGE READING

ASSESSING SECOND LANGUAGE READING

Nooreiny Maarof

PARTRIDGE
A Penguin Random House Company

To order additional copies of this book, contact
Toll Free 800 101 2657 (Singapore)
Toll Free 1 800 81 7340 (Malaysia)
orders.singapore@partridgepublishing.com

www.partridgepublishing.com/singapore

I would like to thank Sharmini Ghanaguru for her kind
assistance in preparation of Chapter 10 of the book

CONTENTS

INTRODUCTION

Assessing Second Language Reading is addressed to both teacher- trainees and to those interested in the teaching and learning of reading in a second or foreign language. It is specifically for teachers who are interested in an alternative method of assessing reader's reading comprehension for both research purposes and classroom use. The book includes a general overview of reading theories and models. It provides a thorough theoretical basis for teachers to understand the comprehension process. An example of how the written recall is used to assess reader's understanding is also included.

The premise of the book is that reading is a constructive and interactive activity whereby the reader constructs meaning based on what he or she already knows about the text and on information within the text. Chapter 1 explicates on the various views of reading comprehension and assessment. Chapter 2 describes basic concepts behind reading models. Chapter 3 describes the three basic types of reading models and explores the concepts of schema and reading. Chapter 4 introduces the reader to the idea of constructivism in second language reading. Chapter 5 discusses factors involved in assessing comprehension. The written recall, an alternative assessment method, is described in Chapter 6. Chapter 7 describes a study which compared the written recall and multiple-choice question tasks. Chapter 8 provides a detailed description of the written recall procedure. Chapter 9 concludes with some recommendations for second language reading pedagogy and research.

I hope the book will be a useful resource for the teacher in his or her attempt to facilitate and understand readers' understanding.

CHAPTER 1

PERSPECTIVES ON READING COMPREHENSION

> ... assessment is infrequently the final act and very frequently Act One or even the prologue to the event of teaching and learning.
>
> - Elizabeth Bernhardt (1996: 191)

Current views of reading comprehension have been largely influenced by constructivist perspectives. The consensus is that reading is an interactive process involving features of readers, texts, and tasks. In particular, the reader is seen as an active participant who constructs meaning from the clues found in printed text (Anderson & Pearson, 1984; Bloome & Greene, 1984; Farr & Carey, 1986; Grabe, 1991; Rumelhart, 1977; Schank, 1984; Spiro, 1980, among others).In this view, readers cease to be *passive tabula rasas* or mere receivers of information. On the contrary, meaning is actively created by the reader as h/she interacts with text. Hence, meaning is not inherent in texts, but rather texts have the potential for meaning (Widdowson, 1979). With the active participation of the reader, reading becomes an individual process that entails different interpretations for different readers. Reading comprehension is thus understood as involving multiple interpretations of text that vary from reader to reader. These differences in reconstructions of meaning are due, in large measure, to the differential amounts of prior knowledge that each reader possesses (Bernhardt, 1991; Carrell, 1983; Langer, 1983; Langer & Nicolich, 1981; Spiro & Myers, 1984; Nuttall, 1996).

The view of the reading process has thus changed from one in which the text has been given prominence to one where the interaction of reader and text is considered most significant. This change in perspective (whereby readers are seen as active participants in the reading process), as evident in the area of reading research, has occurred much like Kuhn's (1970) description of paradigm shifts. In reading research, one of the catalysts for change has been the focus on the reader as one who plays an active role in the reading process (Kamil, 1984). The prevalent constructivist conception of reading comprehension is one that "portrays the reader as actively building a mental representation" (Spivey, 1989, 4) of text through a process of "relating new or incoming information to information already stored in memory" (Bernhardt & James, 1987,3). Changes in models and theories of reading inform us of the processes that are involved in the act-of making meaning from texts. An ideal and desired consequence of that awareness should allow us to base assessments of reading on these changes so that what is understood of the process is reflected in our assessment measures.

Constructivist views of reading assessment emphasize measures that focus on how readers construct meaning (Bernhardt, 1983; Johnston, 1983; Pearson & Valencia, 1987). The interest is on process over product measures. Consequently, researchers are beginning to conduct studies from an insider's or "emic" perspective (Johnston, 1989), an approach characteristic of qualitative sociologists, educational anthropologists, and sociolinguists (Garcia & Pearson, 1991). This shift in approach focusing on how individuals construct meaning has made many educators and researchers realize the inadequacy of a majority of performance measures. As a consequence, the rhetoric of the field of education, in particular the area of reading comprehension, calls for assessment measures that could reveal how readers approach, monitor, and process text.

ASSESSMENT OF READING IN A SECOND/FOREIGN LANGUAGE CONTEXT

Most current assessments of reading comprehension do not reflect the change in perspective about what constitutes reading comprehension. In fact, the prevalent assessment practices and approaches (e.g., multiple-choice tests) are at odds with current theoretical and research-based views of the reading process (Bernhardt, 1991; Winograd, Paris, & Bridge, 1991; Pearson & Valencia, 1987). The existing practices of reading comprehension assessments such as the multiple-choice questions test continue to maintain single, predetermined correct answers. This approach focuses on the evaluation of the number of right or wrong answers only, rather than on the ways readers construct meaning. Furthermore, this conventional approach most often measures only isolated skills and quantity of answers correct (Bernhardt &James, 1987; Winograd, Paris, & Bridge, 1991). Such traditional assessment practice implies that only texts carry meaning, and that all the reader has to do is to extract this meaning. However, research has indicated that reader-based factors, such as prior knowledge, play a more pervasive role in this meaning-making process than the features of text alone (e.g. Allen, Bernhardt, Berry, & Demel, 1988). In this era of accountability, wherein scores of reading tests are used as yardsticks to measure such factors as educational outcomes, schools' effectiveness, and teachers' effectiveness and to make crucial decisions regarding placement (Johnston, 1983; Pearson & Valencia, 1987), there is a need for more theory-based and research-based measures of comprehension. In addition, because reading involves a complex interaction of readers, texts, and tasks, it is important that measures of comprehension are adequately sensitive to capture any effects of such interactions on readers' performance (Davey, 1989).

Furthermore, because reading scores are relied on to make important political, instructional, and placement decisions, it is thus crucial that assessment measures employed need to be not only reliable, valid, and effective measures of reading comprehension, but should also reflect the emerging conception of what research evidence has indicated to be a viable model of the reading process. Reading processes, however, are not directly observable. We can only infer from samples of behaviors assumed to reflect real reading (Farr & Carey, 1986). No single measure could thus capture adequately what readers comprehend from text. The old axiom that reading is a complex process implies that no simplistic measure could reveal the essence of the process. Therefore, several researchers recommend the use of multiple measures or a variety of measures to adequately assess understanding of texts read by using both product and process measures (Aiken, 1987; Bernhardt, 1991; Carrell, Devine, & Eskey, 1988; Garcia & Pearson, 1991;Johnston, 1983; Pearson & Valencia, 1987; among others).

For students in a developing country like Malaysia, the medium of instruction in education is in the national language, *Bahasa Malaysia,* whereas the language of a majority of bibliographical materials remains in English- an official second language. Students therefore deal daily with texts written in the English language in their academic work. They have to read, understand, and often synthesize the information gleaned from English texts into an academic report or paper, which is in turn written in the academic language, *Bahasa Malaysia.* Reading comprehension for these students is thus more than just a matter of answering questions that have a single preselected answer. What these students do in real-life academic reading is not reflected in the assessments that they have been exposed to throughout their earlier education. It is therefore important that assessments of reading comprehension reflect closely the real-life academic reading activity that students engage in everyday; in other words, reading comprehension assessments need to have ecological validity (Fare & Carey, 1986; Johnston, 1983; Spiro & Myers,1984).

There are various assessment approaches to reading comprehension that are in line with the current theoretical and research-based view of what is considered to be the reading process (e.g. the immediate written recall protocol, reading journals, portfolios, etc; See Aebersold & Field, 1997, for a discussion of some alternative assessment methods). There is an urgent need for such approaches to be included in assessments of students' reading comprehension. Because it is often the case that assessments inevitably drive instruction (Aiken, 1987; Jorcey, 1987), assessment approaches implemented should be consistent with theory and research evidence on the reading process. This could lead to a "theoretically sound pedagogy" (Bernhardt & James, 1987, 7). Curriculum designs that include results of assessments to inform, revise, and complement instruction (e.g. Jenks, 1981) are important in promoting effective educational goals. The use of such assessment approaches could complement instruction of reading in a second language. The written recall protocol could provide more than mere quantitative information (i.e. scores). More importantly, it can reveal qualitative information that can be used for diagnostic and instructional purposes. It is important to understand what is involved in the process of reading in order to adequately assess readers' understanding. The next chapter discusses in detail the reading process and the various models of reading.

CHAPTER 2

READING THEORIES AND MODELS

The terms 'theory' and 'model' as used often in the educational literature seem to reflect similar denotations (Kamil, 1986). Nonetheless, they can be distinguished in terms of how each is defined. According to Kamil (1986), a "theory is essentially a representation of what is known to be factual about a set of phenomena" whereas a model assists us "to visualize what it is that we mean by the theory, ..." (p. 71). Lachman (1960, cited in Kamil, 1986) delineated other uses of models: as analogies; to make predictions; to demonstrate the application of a theory; and to help visualize elements and relationships between these elements within an area. Hence, Kamil's description of the terms 'theory' and 'model' can be aptly extended to reading theories and models in that reading models are attempts to depict theories of the reading process.

The history of reading research is said to be about a hundred years old. The focus on building explicit models of the reading process, however, is only a little over three decades old (Samuels & Kamil, 1988). Since the 1960's, however, various changes and improvements have been achieved in model building that attempt to specify the assumed processes involved in the act of reading. Recent models are more precise in describing what could actually occur during the reading process (Athey, 1985). Contributions to the present state of more illuminating descriptions of the reading process have been interdisciplinary. Among some of these domains of knowledge that have contributed to theories and models of reading include cognitive psychology, education, linguistics, psycholinguistics, sociolinguistics, and information-processing.

Because theories and models of the reading process are closely inter-related, most models of reading implicitly reflect the underlying theory that supports them. It is therefore a common practice that one is often used to account for the other. Earlier models can be distinguished from later ones in the focus that each has on how meaning is achieved from print. To assist description of the reading process, theorists and researchers have relied upon metaphors to clarify not only the directionality of creating meaning, but also to indicate the mode preference in processing meaning (Eskey & Grabe, 1988). Hence, the terms "bottom-up", "top-down", and "interactive" are metaphors used in developing models of reading. For instance, "top" refers to higher level "mental concepts such as the knowledge and expectations of the reader" and "bottom" refers to the "physical text on the page"

(Eskey & Grabe, 1988,223). Accordingly, models of reading can be classified into: Bottom-up, Top-down, and Interactive.

BOTTOM-UP MODELS OF READING

Bottom-up models of reading are models that generally assume that the process of reading starts with the print in text. The process begins with the decoding of letters, and the combination of letters into words. Processing then proceeds through a series of stages of clause to phrase to sentence to paragraphs, and finally, to the processing of text (Gough, 1972; Karnil, 1986; Powell, 1988; Samuels & Kamil, 1984). Bottom-up models are also called 'text-based' or 'skills-based' models because of the emphasis on print (Kamil, 1986). The print on the page is decoded into a phonological representation before any assignment of meaning occurs. Bottom-up models are thus linear models where processing occurs in a stage-by-stage fashion without any higher stages influencing lower stages. A classic example of the bottom-up view of reading is Gough's 1972 model, which was formulated during the information- processing era (Samuels & Kamil, 1984).

A limitation of this model is the strict linear processing that does not take into account the possibility of higher processing stages interacting with lower processing stages (Samuels & Kamil, 1984). Goodman (1967), who formulated the first top-down model, characterized the bottom-up model as a notion based upon the common sense view that reading constitutes a precise process; a process that involves exact and detailed identification of letters, words, sentences; moving from smaller units to larger units of language. Other models of the bottom-up type include Carver's 1977-1978 model (cited in Samuels & Kamil, 1984) and LaBerge and Samuels' 1974 model. The LaBerge and Samuels model, like Gough's model, is an information-processing model. As in Gough's model, LaBerge and Samuels assume the reading process as one that occurs in a linear and hierarchical fashion. However, the difference between both models is the focus on 'automaticity' in the processing at lower stages (LaBerge & Samuels, 1974). The limited information- processing capacity of readers is significant to this model. LaBerge and Samuels believe that reading involves the two processes of decoding and comprehension. If extra attention is devoted to decoding, very little or none can be devoted to comprehension. Therefore, according to LaBerge and Samuels, it is necessary for decoding to become automatic so that more attention could be given to comprehension. And only then could fluent reading occur. LaBerge and Samuels have since then enhanced and modified their model to include "feedback loops" (Kamil, 1986, 78). These feedback loops allow processing at some stages to influence other stages.

Carver's 1977-1978 model also belongs to the linear, bottom-up class of models (Kamil, 1986). Carver developed the theory of 'rauding' that accounts for certain aspects of reading. "Rauding" is the process of obtaining meaning from text in a way that each 'thought' is quickly understood

(Kamil, 1986, p. 79). Carver considers such reading skills as skimming, scanning, memorizing and so forth as other behaviors different from rauding. In Carver's view, rauding is dependent upon the difficulty-level of text, the readers' purposes, and the individual reader's ability level (Kamil, 1986). In addition, within this perspective, words are read individually and interpreted in stages. Therefore, in this sense the model is characteristic of bottom-up models. Kamil (1986) concurs that this model is important because it stresses many elements of the reacting process that are overlooked in other models, and also for the implications that it holds for instruction.

A limitation of all these linear, bottom-up models is the strict sequential processing that is assumed to occur with the absence of any lower stages influencing and interacting with other higher processing stages (Samuels & Kamil, 1984). Each stage is thus dependent upon the previous stage. None of these models could explain well the processing that occurs at the discourse level; that is, what actually happens when we comprehend whole texts, or when comprehension occurs.

TOP-DOWN MODELS OF READING

Top-down models of reading assume that the process of meaning-making begins with the knowledge that readers have in their heads. Readers are conceived as less textbound than is assumed by the bottom- up models (Kamil, 1986). These models suggest that readers begin the reading process by making guesses about the meaning of the text being read. Reading therefore involves making predictions about the print in text. Based upon the fewest cues in text, readers construct meaning with the guidance of prior knowledge that readers possess about the text. Goodman (976) describes reading as follows:

> Reading is a selective process. It involves partial use of available minimal language cues selected from perceptual input on the basis of the reader's expectation. As this partial information is processed, tentative decisions are made to be confirmed, rejected, or refined as reading progresses. More simply stated, reading is a psycholinguistic guessing game. It involves an interaction between thought and language. Efficient reading does not result from precise perception and identification of all elements, but from skill in selecting the fewest, most productive cues necessary to produce guesses which are right the first time. (p. 260)

From this perspective, fluent readers form hypotheses, make predictions, sample text based on minimal visual cues, and confirm or reject predictions using information in text and prior knowledge. Smith (1988), another proponent of the top-down model, views reading as one of the many things that we do to "make sense of the world" (p. x). He further asserts that meaning is not in the text, but is reader inherent. He names this reader-based information "non-visual information" as opposed to "visual information" that "goes away when the lights go out" (Smith, 1988, 65). Sharing Goodman's perspective, Smith considers this non-visual information or background knowledge essential for fluent reading. He quotes Kolers (1969, 67), "Reading is only incidently visual", to convince readers that central to reading is this non-visual information.

Top-down models thus emphasize higher-order cognitive processes involving the association of meaning to print, not vice-versa, as in earlier bottom-up models. Goodman's model, better known as the "psycholinguistic guessing game" model has had a profound influence on reading instruction, especially in reading instruction of children (Samuels & Kamil, 1988). In the area of reading research, the influence of Goodman's model can clearly be seen in the number of citations of the model (251 citations) in studies and articles devoted to reading in native language and second language between the years 1974 to 1988 (Bernhardt, 1991, pp. 24-25). Among educators in second language reading, this top-down model has achieved close to an official status as the model that describes the reading process (Eskey, 1986). Goodman's model is based upon miscue analysis or the detection of errors in oral reading. Based on this analysis, a model is built to infer as to what occurs during reading.

Critics of the top-down models point to the importance of knowledge of the language (perceptual and decoding skills of print) as critical to the understanding of text (Carrell & Eisterhold, 1988; Eskey, 1986; Grabe, 1986). Top-down models seem to deemphasize the importance of bottom-up decoding skills. Although language serves as a 'skeleton, a blueprint for the creation of meaning' (Spiro, 1980, 245), limited knowledge of decoding print and of language in general will not allow readers to see the blueprint to create meaning. This seems to be the thrust of the argument against a strong top-down view of reading in which lower level skills are given less importance. Eskey (1986) argues that the model promoted in top-down models is that of a skilful, fluent reader whose lower-order skills (perceptual and decoding skills) have become automatized.

INTERACTIVE MODELS OF READING

Interactive models of reading combine aspects of both bottom-up and top-down models. Reading is described as involving a simultaneous processing of information -neither directionally nor hierarchically- that occurs at various levels. Interactive models assume an interaction between higher level and lower level knowledge structures. Rumelhart's 1977 model initiated the formulations of models that belong to the interactive classification. Rumelhart (1980) later incorporated ideas from schema theory into his interactive model, thus making it more plausible and insightful in explaining the process of reading. The interactive model emphasizes flexible processing, which involves multiple knowledge sources. Information that readers bring to bear upon text combines with the information in the text itself. Reading, therefore, does not become an exercise of extracting information. Rather it becomes a communication act-a dialogue-between the reader and text (Grabe, 1988; Widdowson, 1979). Widdowson (1979) suggests that meaning is not inherent in text; instead text has the potential for meaning.

Interactive models seem to strike a better balance between the many subprocesses of reading (Eskey, 1988). These models do not assume the primacy of top-down processing, that is, the steady replacing of decoding of each individual word with educated guesses (guesses based on the least amount of visual cues). Instead, interactive models posit the dynamic interaction between bottom-up and top-down processing. From this perspective, "good readers are both good decoders and good interpreters of texts, their decoding skills becoming more automatic but no less important ..." (Eskey, 1988, 94).

Stanovich (1980) argues that bottom-up and top-down models do not describe the reading process well. He points to the lack of feedback where higher level processes could influence lower level processes and vice-versa. For instance, sentence-context effects and prior knowledge of topic that could help word recognition and, eventually, comprehension are not accounted for in the earlier models (Kamil, 1984). Stanovich advanced the interactive-compensatory model, which he considers to be the current model of what constitutes reading. According to him, within the interactive-compensatory model, processing at one level can compensate for weaknesses at other levels. Hence, per this model, a reader who lacks background knowledge of the topic or content of text, but has good decoding skills can make-up for the lack of knowledge through use of bottom-up processing. On the contrary, if the reader is weak in decoding skills, s/he can rely more on top-down, conceptual knowledge to comprehend what is read.

Most current models of the reading process are of the interactive type (e.g., Bernhardt, 1985; Coady, 1979; Perfetti, 1985). Even Goodman (1988) has alluded to the fact that his psycholinguistic guessing game model has always acknowledged the role of bottom-up skills. However, he contends that conceptual or background knowledge plays a more significant role in the reading process. Coady (1979) advanced his psycholinguistic model for EFL/ESL reading which is similar to Stanovich's model, in that weaknesses at one level-whether at the level of decoding skills and language, or at the level of background or prior knowledge could compensate for weaknesses at other levels. In particular, Coady suggests that background knowledge could compensate for some syntactic weaknesses. However, he points out that the inclusion of high interest materials related to the readers' background is a concomitance for this compensatory mechanism to operate efficiently.

SUMMARY

Reading theories and models, in general, are attempts to describe the complex process of reading. Recent theories and models have been influenced to some extent by previous ones. Emerging views of what constitutes the process of reading have become more precise and insightful due to the accumulation of empirical evidences that help support the theories and models posited. Nonetheless, these models remain partial models (Kamil, 1986). As yet, "there is no model, psycholinguistic or linguistic, that is adequate to explain reading" (Athey, 1985,58). Because of this inadequacy of models in fully explaining the reading process, some educators consider them of limited usefulness. Athey (1985) points to the fact that the complexity of the reading process is responsible for the limited usefulness of models, not the models' inadequacies. However, theories and models of the reading process have implications for instruction. Theories and models can assist us in the attempt to fully understand a complex phenomenon such as the reading process.

Crucial to an understanding of the reading process is the concept of background knowledge or schema theory. The next chapter is an overview of schema theory and its role in the comprehension of texts.

CHAPTER 3

SCHEMA THEORY AND READING

Central to reading theories and models of reading is the notion of "schema". Some definitions of schema (plural is schemata) are: a description of a specific class of concepts that is made up of a hierarchy of other schemata (Adams & Collins, 1985); the organized knowledge that we have of the world (Anderson, 1985); a knowledge structure or the knowledge that is stored in our memory (Anderson & Pearson, 1988); the knowledge structure that we have previously acquired (Carrell & Eisterhold, 1988); linguistic knowledge and background knowledge structures termed critical mass (Devine, 1988); data structure that represents concepts of a general nature that are stored in memory (Rumelhart, 1980).

Thus, a consensus description of schemata is that they are knowledge structures that we have about events, experiences, and so forth. In short, schemata are knowledge structures of the world. In reading, schemata include knowledge of the text (its contents) and the background knowledge that we have about the topic (Carrell, Devine, & Eskey, 1988; Eskey, 1986). In all models of the reading process, whether bottom-up, top-down, or interactive, the notion of schemata or knowledge structures is central to an understanding of the process of reading. These knowledge structures such as knowledge of print, the language, and knowledge that we have in our heads about the topic form a framework that guide the construction of meaning from texts (Adams & Collins, 1985; Anderson, Reynolds, Schallert, & Goetz, 1977; Bartlett, 1932; Rumelhart, 1980; among others). Other terms used to refer to schema or schemata include scripts and plans (Schank & Abelson, 1975); frames (Minsky, 1975 cited in Powell, 1988); event chains (Warren, Nicholas, &Trabasso, 1979); and critical mass (Eskey, 1986).

The notion of schema is associated with studies conducted by Sir Frederic Bartlett (1932). Bartlett contended that past experiences have an influential role in the process of comprehending and remembering texts. However, he maintained that memories are reconstructed upon recollection, and that they are based upon schema, rather than the notion that memory is mere retrieval of information from a storehouse of traces of past happenings (Wilson & Anderson, 1986). Bartlett thus does not consider schema as involving the notion of storage; rather his reference to schema is used in a "functional-phenomenal sense" (Iran-Nejad, 1987, 122). That is, to Bartlett, a schema is active and transcient. Schemata are being built-up all the time while being influenced by information of past experiences. This is evident in his statement that "... to serve the needs of biological adaptation interests are all the while increasing in diversity, in narrowness and in definiteness. So our range of search, when we attempt recall, tends to get more and more refined..." (Bartlett, 1932,312).

Bartlett's idea of schema and his use of the text as a template, against which recalls are compared for any changes in readers' constructions are characteristics of contemporary constructivist tradition (Spivey: 1989). Although Bartlett's works are associated with the notion of schema, the idea has long been acknowledged within works of the Gestalt psychologists (Anderson & Pearson, 1988). Gestalt psychology underlines the Significance of "holistic properties" and is concerned with "mental organization" (Anderson & Pearson, 1988, 38). To the Gestalt psychologists, the whole experience cannot be inferred from its parts.

Gestalt psychology has been adopted in studies on visual memory and perception, and has provided Support for the notion of the influence of schemata on comprehending and remembering texts (Anderson & Pearson, 1988). Ausabel (1963, cited in Anderson & Pearson, 1988; Wilson & Anderson, 1986; Spiro, 1980; LaZansky, Spencer, & Johnston, 1987), a prominent figure in education and psychology shares similar views with that of Bartlett and the Gestalt psychologists. Ausubel advanced the idea of how meaningful learning is dependent upon the inter-connectivity between new ideas and a learner's established prior knowledge (Anderson & Pearson, 1988; Brown, 1987; LaZansky, Spencer, & Johnston, 1987). That is, general prior knowledge subsume(s) or anchor(s) the new information in the text read (Anderson & Pearson, 1988, 41). Ausubel introduced the idea of advance organizers, or organizers that serve as a scaffold to bridge the gap between what a reader knows (prior knowledge) and the new information encountered in text (Wilson &Anderson, 1986; Brown, 1987).

The historical figures discussed in the preceding paragraphs share the central idea that schema is a factor that underlies any description of reading and comprehension of texts. Comprehending and remembering are found to be influenced by what readers know about the text (e.g., content, genre, language, and cultural knowledge). The notion of schemata is thus relevant to both reading in a native language and in a second language. Although schemata are not the only factors involved in the reading process, they however help to explain how we interpret new information as we read, and how this new information becomes part of the knowledge structures we possess. Current views of the reading process define reading as this interaction of new information with the old knowledge (knowledge that we already possess).

To reiterate, schema theory helps us understand how what people know affects how and what they comprehend (Wilson & Anderson, 1986). An insightful description of a schema is that it is an "abstract structure of knowledge ... structured in the sense that it indicates relations among constituent concepts ... abstract in the sense that one schema has the potential to cover a number of texts that differ in particulars." (Wilson &Anderson, 1986,33). These concepts that constitute a schema contain "slots" that can be "instantiated" with information in text (Anderson & Pearson,

1988; Rumelhart, 1980; Spiro, 1980; Wilson & Anderson, 1986). Thus, according to schema theory, every kind of information is "mapped" against some already existing information or schema, and everything about that schema must fit the new information (Carrell & Eisterhold, 1988, p. 76).

Studies by Schank and Abelson (1977) and Anderson, Spiro, and Anderson (1978) illustrate how certain specific information can instantiate particular slots within a schema. Carrell and Eisterhold (1988) postulate that the process of interpretation, guided by the principle of schema theory, results in top-down and bottom-up processing. The incoming data or input become the catalyst for bottom-up processing. Bottom-up processing is therefore said to be data-driven (Carrell & Eisterhold, 1988). When lower-level schemata interact or converge with higher-level schemata, these higher level general schemata are activated. Top-down processing that involves conceptually-driven schemata occurs when predictions based upon higher level general schemata operate, and later converge with lower level schemata (Carrell, Devine, & Eskey, 1988).

The view that reading involves an active reader as participant in the reading process is first recognized in first or native language reading (Carrell, 1988), and it is over the past two decades that this view is prevalent in second and foreign language reading (Bernhardt, 1986; Carrell, 1983, 1988; Clarke & Silberstein, 1977; Coady, 1979; Eskey, 1973; Grabe, 1991; Hudson, 1982; Johnson, 1981; Steffensen, Joag-dev, & Anderson, 1979). The interactive view of reading, both referring to processing mode (interaction of various component skills in parallel processing) and interaction of reader and text-(the reader constructs meaning based on knowledge from text and existing prior knowledge), has had a strong influence on both reading in a native language and reading in a second language. These interactive views of reading have become influential in research and instruction with the inclusion of schema theory to support the significance and impact of prior knowledge-whether linguistic knowledge or knowledge about the world-on readers' comprehension of texts.

The intuitive appeal of schema theory and its instructional implications (e.g., prereading exercises, semantic mapping) has prompted much research on schema theory over the past decade (Grabe, 1991). Research by Alderson and Urquhart (1988), Carrell (1984b, 1987), Carrell & Eisterhold (1988), and Hudson (1982), among others, provide evidence of the effects of schemata (formal, content, or linguistic) on the process of comprehending second language texts.

Schema theory is not without its criticisms, however. Some researchers and theorists in the area of reading point to the abstractness of schema theory. The argument is that schema theory is not well-defined to be used as a framework to represent how knowledge is structured (Grabe, 1991). There are those who contend that schemata are not permanent structures capable of being stored, searched, and retrieved from memory, rather they are dynamic and constantly changing (IranNejad, 1986). Despite the criticisms, the notion of a schema has been advantageous to reading research and instruction. Although schema theory cannot be used to explain all the processes involved in reading, schema theory however, provides a succinct and plausible description on how readers' prior knowledge is "integrated in memory and used in higher-level comprehension processes" (Grabe, 1991,390).

CHAPTER 4

CONSTRUCTIVISM AND THE SECOND LANGUAGE MODEL OF READING

For the past decade, the area of reading in a first language has been dominated by constructivist views of reading (Bridge, 1987; Garcia & Pearson, 1991; Johnston, 1983; Seda, 1989; Spivey, 1989). In like manner, constructivist views of reading have had a profound influence on research and instruction in reading in a second and foreign language (Berkemeyer, 1989; Connor, 1984; Hague, 1989; Hammadou, 1988, 1991; Lee, 1986, 1990; Lee & Riley, 1990; Steffensen, Joag-dev & Anderson, 1979;Wells, 1986;Wolff, 1987).

Constructivism depicts the reader as an active participant in the reading process-in building a mental representation-by relating new, incoming information in text with old information or previously acquired knowledge (Bernhardt, 1986, 1991; Pearson & Valencia, 1987; Collins, Brown, & Larkin, 1980; Johnston, 1983; Spiro, 1980; Spivey, 1989; Wixson & Peters, 1987). Thus, from this view, reading involves actively combining what one knows with what is in the text. The meaning of what is read depends upon the reader's interpretations. The reader plays an important role in the construction of meaning. The reader reconstructs the meaning of the text read from his/her own understanding. Consequently, this implies that meaning does not reside in the text. Widdowson (1979), among other researchers, attests to this in his suggestion that texts do not carry meaning.

This constructive activity necessarily involves top-down and bottom- up processing in an interactive mode. Bartlett's use of schema theory and texts as templates to compare recalls is adopted by many constructivist researchers and educators in the area of reading today (Spivey, 1989). In this approach, researchers attempt to discover and understand the nature of the readers' construction of meaning.

RADICAL CONSTRUCTIVISM

Although Bartlett's (1932) work is acknowledged as the impetus for research in reading in the constructivist tradition, there are other historical thinkers and philosophers who deserve mention as influential sources of the idea of constructivism. It should be noted that many researchers and theorists in reading have not explicitly acknowledged the particular sources of constructivist influence on their ideas and works. However, many of the ideas of these researchers as displayed in their work reflect certain characteristics of the ideas of radical constructivism (e.g., Bernhardt, 1983, 1985, 1991, among others). In many ways, constructivist views in the area of reading can be related to some of the ideas of radical constructivism. A contemporary radical constructivist, whose discussions of the ideas of constructivism and its implications for education are both illuminating and cogent, is von Glasersfeld (1988, 1989a, 1989b). In his explication of constructivism, he acknowledges his debt to past philosophers and thinkers such as Bogdanov (1909), Vico (1710), Bentham (1760), Kant (1787), and in particular to Piaget (1937), who he considers the pioneer of today's constructivist idea of knowing (cited in von Glasersfeld, 1988, 1989a, 1989b).

Radical constructivism is a theory of epistemology that runs counter to that of traditional theory of knowledge. Basic to the radical constructivist theory of knowing is the idea that "knowledge is a mapping of ways of acting and thinking and the result of an individuals own cognitive activity, and not a commodity residing outside the knower that can be conveyed by linguistic communication." (von Glasersfeld, 1988, 1). On the contrary, the traditional epistemological theory assumes that knowledge is called true if it can reflect an accurate representation of a world that exists "in itself", prior to and independent of the knower's experience of it". (von Glasersfeld, 1989a, 4). Von Glasersfeld (1988) postulates that radical constructivism is a theory of knowing rather than a theory of knowledge. He further explained that it is radical because it differs radically from traditional theories of knowledge.

There are four key ideas of radical constructivism: (a) the Sceptics' contentions; (b) of Scientific Truth; (c) the Nature of Concepts; and (d) the idea of Adaptation. Radical constructivism integrates these four central ideas, and in so doing, discounts the traditional proposal of veridical knowledge, and is thus incompatible with traditional dogma of true knowledge (von Glasersfeld, 1988). The first key idea of radical constructivism concerns the assumption of the Sceptics, whose ideas form the root of constructivism. The Sceptics' realization that it is not possible for us to be certain of real world knowledge because even if we could discover knowledge through experience, we can never discover how this experience is related to what exists before we experience it. This idea is based on the assumption that the knowledge we have must have been derived from our own experience, that is through our senses, actions, and thoughts (von Glasersfeld, 1989b). Hence, we have no means of checking the truth of our knowledge with the world that is beyond our experiential world.

Plato, an influential historical philosopher, claimed that some God had planted the "pure ideas" in us and that experience with the unclear, less than perfect world makes us recollect what was really true (von Glasersfeld, 1989b, 2). This awareness of the state of true knowledge was inherent from the Pre-Socratic age to the Byzantium theologians in 4th century A.D. (von Glasersfeld, 1989a). The Byzantium theologians affirmed "the absolute transcendence of God and excluded any possibility of identifying Him with any human concept ... for no human word or thought is capable of comprehending what God is." (Meyendorff, 1974, cited in von Glasersfeld, 1989a, 3). This idea of the limitation of human understanding was adhered to and generalized by sceptics of later ages such as Montaigne, Marsenne, Berkeley, Hume, and finally to Kant who formulated these ideas in his *Critique of Pure Reason* in 1787 (von Glasersfeld, 1988).

The second key idea of radical constructivism concerns the state of scientific truth. The theologians, Osiander and Cardinal Bellarmino, asserted that scientific knowledge should not be a reflection of the real world, only that science should be seen as an instrument in predicting experiences, but "must never claim to capture God's truth" (von Glasersfeld, 1989a, 3). These theologians posited this idea to protect their faith from being undermined by arguments of the sceptics and science. Von Glasersfeld points out that they laid the foundation of instrumentalism; that is, the proposal that scientific and rational knowledge serve as if ... an *instrumental* function in the living organisms' management of their subjective experiential reality." (von Glasersfeld, 1989a, 20).

The nature of concepts or cognitive construction forms the third key idea of radical constructivism. This idea was first suggested by the Italian philosopher, Giambattista Vico (1710, cited in von Glasersfeld, 1989a). In his phrase 'God is the artificer of man, man is the god of artifacts', he alludes to the idea that for us to know something is to know the nature of what that thing is in the first place. Hence, God alone can have knowledge of the real world, for it was God who created it. Accordingly, we humans can know only what we have constructed (von Glasersfeld, 1989a). To Vico, facts are the "experiential elements out of which organisms 'make' ... or construct their experiential worlds, ..." (von Glasersfeld, 1989a, 20).

The final key idea of the radical constructivists concerns the concept of adaptation. This concept was adopted from Darwin's theory of evolution, and is used in the attempt to explain the evolution of knowledge. Therefore, concepts within Darwin's theory of evolution such as *"variation, selection, adaptation,* and *viability"* (von Glasersfeld, 1989a, 20) are applied to the area of cognition. For instance, knowledge is seen as traceable by using Darwin's central concept of natural selection and adaptation. Darwin's concept of fit is used as an alternative to traditional concepts of knowledge. In this sense, the function of human cognition is viewed as "adaptive, in the biological sense of the term, tending towards fit or *viability"* (von Glasersfeld, 1989b, 5).

Radical constructivism sees the experiential world of humans as something constructed-a result of the thinking human's own "distinguishing and relating"-that began with the individuals making distinctions between the self and the experiential world (von Glasersfeld, 1989a, 20). Von Glasersfeld argues that radical constructivism does not "deny ontological reality" (p. 20), it merely argues that man or the cognizing organisms cannot come to know any ontologically real world because what man knows has been derived from his experiences in life.

Radical constructivists' ideas on environment and communication, which are relevant to contemporary constructivist ideas in reading, are also derived from the four key ideas of radical constructivism. To radical constructivists, environment and communication are subjective constructs of humans (von Glasersfeld, 1988). It is further assumed that knowledge is not acquired in large amounts, rather it must be accumulated from parts that are often small, basic pieces. Von Glasersfeld reminds us that there is nothing novel about the notion that students have to construct knowledge based on their experience in the form of teacher's discourse, a textbook, or their own world knowledge.

In education, general and specific models of students' cognitive construction are often made. These models are regarded by realists to be a reflection of what students really are. On the contrary, constructivists are aware that models mirror only the model builder's conceptual constructs based on what the model builder considers reality as s/he has experienced it. Nonetheless, constructivists emphasize that one's conceptual constructing is not arbitrary for it is "constantly held in check by the constraints it runs into" (von Glasersfeld, 1988,7).

The task of spoonfeeding students with ready-made knowledge is no longer seen to be the responsibility of education. Instead, it is the task for the educators to infer possible models of students' conceptual constructs, and thereafter attempt hypotheses regarding how students could be given the opportunity to modify their cognition so as to be compatible with the teacher's expectations and aims. In this sense, the concept of environment is significant to constructivists. The environment that teachers create should be such that the constraints set up are ones that could lead the students to "propitious accommodations" (von Glasersfeld, 1988,7); that is, the teachers should be able to set up tasks and conditions that could facilitate understanding of a particular subject that a student is attempting to learn. The constructivists emphasize that the environment must never draw upon the assumption that what is obvious to the teacher would be obvious to the student (von Glasersfeld, 1988). Although this idea was meant to refer specifically to mathematics education, it can be extended to all education in general.

Communication to radical constructivists is subjective. This idea of the subjectivity of communication is captured succinctly in Claude Shannon's work on communication (1948, cited in von Glasersfeld, 1988). von Glasersfeld wrote that in Shannon's view, "the physical signals that pass between communicators-for instance the sounds of speech or the visual patterns of print or writing-do not carry what is ordinarily called 'meaning'. Instead, they carry instructions to select particular meanings from a list ... together with the list of convened signals, constitutes the communication code." (p.8). In addition, Shannon points out that if the receiver does not have the lists of codes before the interaction occurs, the signals become meaningless for the receiver. Since linguistic meaning is subjective to constructivists, the notion that words convey ideas or knowledge cannot be maintained. If we understand what another is saying, it does not mean that we have identical structures to the speaker. Instead, the constructivists' contention is that understanding is always "a matter of fit rather than match" (von Glasersfeld, 1988, 11).

In everyday communication between proficient interlocutors, idiosyncracies of cognitive construction often are not apparent. However, when two speakers talk about abstract topics, we often notice discrepancies that will clearly surface. Von Glasersfeld (1988) suggests that if a constructivist position is adopted by the communicators, a more flexible and accommodating attitude would result in the communication act. The speakers will assume that meanings are subjective constructs, and thus will be able to accommodate-and adapt to each other's views.

On the contrary, if a traditional attitude towards communication is taken, the participants will think of their own meaning of words as fixed, unambiguous entities that could lead to an unproductive confrontation. In this sense, an advantage of the radical constructivists' orientation is the resulting tolerance in social interactions. This tolerance is due to "the realization that neither problems nor solutions are ontological entities, but arise from particular ways of constructing." (von Glasersfeld, 1989a, 22). This awareness of the subjectivity of interpretations of language will assist teachers in realizing that there is more than one plausible and reasonable interpretation to any kind of instruction the teacher provides. For instance, if a student's answer is not compatible with that of the teacher's answer, this may not be necessarily proof that the student has committed a logical error. The response maybe perfectly sensible to the student because the concepts that h/she perceives may be different from those that seem obvious to the teacher.

In this instance, Von Glasersfeld (1988) maintains that it would be of little use to inform the student that h/she is wrong. What the teacher should do is to attempt to infer a viable model of the student's conceptual structures, regardless of how bizarre the student's conceptions are. It is only thus that the teacher can locate where the student is conceptually; and consequently, the teacher can devise ways and means that could help the student make accommodations towards a more desirable end.

The current view of reading, in the area of reading in a first or second language, embodies some of the general ideas of radical constructivism. Some of these ideas as applied to reading include: (a) the emphasis on the reader as an active participant who constructs a mental representation of the text in the reading process; (b) the idea that text or words do not carry meaning; (c) the awareness that there are multiple interpretations of text based upon each individuals state of knowledge; (d) the assertion that knowledge is actively built up by the reader, and thus the reader is not a *tabula rasa,* passively receiving information in text; (e) the contention that reading involves the interaction of multiple sources of knowledge (schemata), which leads to preference for the interactive models of reading; (f) the realization that readers are dependent upon the knowledge they possess, and that this knowledge is a result of experience; and (g) knowledge readers gained from experience is brought to bear upon texts when they read to comprehend.

Constructivism, in general, is regarded as a cognitive revolution in most fields of study (Farr & Carey, 1986; Spivey, 1989; Kamil, 1984). Constructivism offers a new and viable perspective of theory and research in the area of reading. Even the conception of literacy has been affected (Carson,

Carrell, Silberstein, Kroll, & Kuehn, 1990). For instance, constructivist ideas have been facilitative in making us aware of the inter-relatedness of reading and writing (Stotsky, 1983; Grabe, 1991). Because reading and writing involve the construction of meaning, they thus share some similar processes (Bartholomae & Petrosky, 1986; Carrell & Connor, 1991; Rubin & Hansen, 1986). As it is today, constructivism has had a dramatic impact on issues of readability of texts, assessment of reading comprehension, reading instruction, and literacy understanding in the United States and internationally (Spivey, 1990). Constructivist perspectives on reading are able to offer viable and beneficial pedagogical implications, as evidenced by numerous studies over the past decade that have been conducted using the constructivist framework.

THE CONSTRUCTIVIST MODEL OF SECOND LANGUAGE READING

A model of reading in a second language that reflects constructivist theory of reading is Bernhardt's (1986) "Constructivist Model" of reading. Bernhardt has not acknowledged radical constructivism as an influence in her work on reading. However, much of her research and work on reading in a second and foreign language reflects some of the ideas of radical constructivism. For instance, Bernhardt's model of second language reading embodies the radical constructivist idea of the active role of the reader in constructing meaning. In addition, the radical constructivist contention that texts do not carry meaning, and that readers bring to the reading process knowledge that they have accumulated through experience can be seen in the theory that underlies the model.

Bernhardt's model is based upon Coady's (1979) model of reading in a second language. It is also similar to Rumelhart's (1977) model in that the components are interactive in nature (Bernhardt, 1986). Thus, the model embodies a schema-theoretic view of reading. Bernhardt's model attempts to account for the constructive process involved in reading for meaning (Lee, 1990). Bernhardt's definition of reading comprehension is the current conception of reading among a majority of reading scholars, namely that reading is "the process of relating new or incoming information to information already stored in memory" (1985, p. 21). Reading involves making associations through "taking units of language and building them into a configuration" (Bernhardt, 1985, 22). This built-up configuration is comprehension, and the mental representation that the reader constructs is known as a discourse model (Bernhardt, 1987).

Bernhardt's model, like Goodman's (1988) model is data-based while Goodman's model was based on miscue analysis, Bernhardt's model was formulated by recall protocol data derived from intermediate college level readers of German, French, and Spanish (Bernhardt, 1986). The model has been tested with first year learners of Spanish, and is found to have "explanatory adequacy" and "predictive capability" (Lee, 1990, 141). In the analysis of his subjects' written recall protocols, Lee (1990) found that their comprehension is a consequence of the interaction of text-based and extra-text based factors. Parallel with findings of previous studies conducted by Bernhardt (1983, 1985), Lee found that the constructivist model could indeed explain the factors involved in readers' construction of meaning. The model is thus able to account for what is already known, in addition to the capability of incorporating findings of previous research (Lee, 1990). The components of the model, as explicated by Bernhardt (1985), are as follows:

> The components of the model are text-based and extra text-based in nature. The three text-based components are word-recognition, phonemic/graphemic decoding, and syntactic feature recognition. Word is defined as the attachment of a semantic value .... Phonemic/graphemic decoding is defined as the recognition of words based on sound or visual mismatch .... Syntactic feature recognition is defined as the relationship between words.
>
> Extratext-based components include intratextual perception, prior knowledge, and metacognition. Intratextual perception concerns the reconciliation of each part of the text with that which precedes and succeeds .... Prior knowledge taps whether the discourse is sensible within the reader's knowledge about the world, ... Metacognition refers to the extent to which the reader is thinking about what he is reading. (p. 25)

Bernhardt's (1983, 1985, 1986, 1987) constructivist model of second language reading was developed from her analyses of students' miscomprehension as evidenced in their written recall protocols. The protocol analysis revealed patterns of "intrusions, distortions, and omissions" (Berkemeyer, 1989, 132) that serve as valuable information on the comprehension process. Based on her analyses of how the students construct meaning of the texts read, Bernhardt formulated the six components of her model. The focus of the model is on the interaction of the various components of the model; that is between the various textual features and the non-textual features. Thus, Bernhardt asserts that proficient reading is dependent upon several interacting factors; factors that combine and interact in a dynamic way in the comprehension process as supported by evidence from her study (Bernhardt, 1987).

Some factors she considers important to comprehension are the "micro elements" of texts (e.g., recognition of inflectional endings), the initial decisions that readers form regarding the topic of the text, and the constant monitoring or thinking of one's understanding (metacognition) as meaning is being constructed (Bernhardt, 1987, 5). Bernhardt (1985) points out that the model reflects the interactive process between multisources of factors. Therefore, she affirms that it is difficult to ascertain in reconstruction which component influences another component. For instance, prior knowledge can influence word recognition, and word recognition can activate or instantiate prior knowledge. The point where the cycle begins cannot be determined. Furthermore, it starts differently for different readers. Hence, the model is said to be three dimensional (Bernhardt, 1985, 1986).

Bernhardt advocates the use of the written recall procedure in assessing comprehension and lists several advantages of using the written recall procedure in assessing comprehension of texts read (1983, 1991). These advantages will be further discussed in the following section under "Comprehension Assessment". However, one significant advantage she stresses concerns the nature of written recall; it reflects process rather than mere product. The technique does not only reveal the content of what is read, but also more importantly, it shows how the readers construct meaning. Bernhardt points out that the written recall technique of testing comprehension is able to avoid many of the pitfalls of traditional tests (e.g., tests such as the multiple-choice and the doze).

CHAPTER 5

READING COMPREHENSION ASSESSMENT

Reading is one of the most important skills in the field of education (Alderson, 1984; Eskey, 1973; Farr & Carey, 1987; Johns, 1981; Ostler, 1980; Schulz, 1983; Tan & Ling, 1979). It is also one of the most often assessed skills (Farr & Carey, 1987; Lim, 1976; Wixson & Peters, 1987). Within the education system of Malaysia itself, a child who begins his/her education from standard one (grade one) through forms five (approximately grade eleven) would have gone through three major national (standardized) examinations (Information Malaysia, 1989; Educational Planning and Research Division, 1985). This is not taking into consideration the numerous tests and quizzes, mid-terms and final examinations at each grade level. These assessments are frequently in the form of reading tests. Reading is therefore a crucial skill for these students, and in particular, reading in a second language (English) for students at the tertiary education level, because most of the reference materials students encounter in their academic endeavor are written in the second language.

Perspectives on what constitutes reading has changed over the last fifteen years (Bernhardt, 1988; Johnston, 1983, 1984). However, this change in view is not apparent in the area of current reading assessment (Bernhardt, 1991;Winograd, Paris, & Bridge, 1991). Assessments of reading comprehension in school curricula maintain traditional approaches, which are in conflict with insights and innovations of recent theories and research on the reading process (pearson & Valencia, 1987; Spivey, 1989).

This disparity has been brought about, at least in the United States, by various reasons. One reason is attributed to the dilemma that teachers face in implementing theory and research-based instruction of reading (Pearson & Valencia, 1987). Tests that are in conflict with current views of reading still drive the curriculum, and teachers are affected by students' poor performance on standardized examinations. Teachers are held accountable for students' performance, and, as a consequence, teachers are "forced to try to integrate two diametrically opposed curricula-one based upon what is measured by tests ... and one based on ... recent research" (Pearson & Valencia, 1987, p. 7).

Pearson and Valencia (1987) point to the irony that in this era, where we are aware of the disparity between existing reading tests and what we know about reading, these very tests are, however, gaining in popularity. There are those who have resorted to the "If we can't beat them, join them" attitude, where the pragmatic option that one can take is to try and improve on the existing traditional tests. For example, Jorcey (1987) advocates the teaching of test-taking strategies (how to perform on multiple-choice tests) as one way to deal with the disparity between reading lessons that go by new insights into reading processes and the reality of students' having to face public examinations- examinations that subscribe to traditional ideas of testing. Jorcey seems to favor the perspective that tests should drive instruction, and implies that past examination papers that provide practice for students are indispensable.

As mentioned earlier, the emerging view of reading is that it is an interactive process between readers and texts, and that it involves the reader's active construction of a mental representation of what is read and understood from text. Although there are various other versions of what is considered reading, the consensus seems to be that the ultimate aim of reading is comprehension (Farr & Carey, 1986). There have been several attempts by researchers and educators interested in the assessment of reading comprehension to define reading comprehension. Johnston (1983) suggests that to develop a definition of comprehension, issues of whether comprehension is seen as a process or product should first be considered. That is, should comprehension be viewed as "the change in (or state of) knowledge which has occurred ... or as the process by which the change (or state) comes about?" (Johnston, 1983, 2).

Most current assessment approaches to reading comprehension in education assume that reading comprehension is a product of the reader's interaction with what is read (Perkins & Parish, 1988; Myers, 1991; Sternberg, 1991). The meaning that is reconstructed as a result of this interaction can be examined by asking readers to express their understandings (Johnston, 1983), for instance, by asking readers to answer questions. Johnston concurs that this approach emphasizes the final products, rather than the process or processes involved in understanding. Myers (1991) considers both product and process approaches as pertinent to the assessment of reading comprehension. Although recent research findings emphasize the process approach over the product approach, Myers points to the Significance of using information of processes of reading that could improve comprehension as a product. He therefore recommends the use of product measures to support process measures to derive "converging evidence of the degree to which indices of process measures ... correlate with product measures ..." (Myers, 1991, 264).

COMPREHENSION AND MEMORY

An issue that relates to the process and product views of comprehension is the type of memory processes that are involved with each view of comprehension. Carroll (1971, cited in Johnston, 1983) contends that comprehension involves only short-term memory. According to Carroll, comprehension immediately occurs upon reception of information, and that once longer time intervals are used in tests, we are testing memory processes together with or instead of comprehension processes. Carroll thus advocates the assessment of comprehension immediately upon presentation of a passage. On the contrary, Royer and Cunningham (1981) posit that comprehension processes and memory processes are interrelated. Their definition of a comprehended message is concerned with the representation of the message in memory, and they assume that "a comprehended message will be retained in memory better than an uncomprehended message." (Royer & Cunningham, 1981, p. 208). Several studies provide evidence supporting this assumption (e.g., Bransford & Johnson, 1972; Steffensen, Joag-dev, & Anderson, 1979; Eskey, 1986).

Similarly, Voss, Tyler, and Bisanz (1982), in their review of the literature on prose comprehension and memory, maintained that comprehension and memory effects are inseparable. They argue that if comprehension were to be measured immediately after the presentation of text, this would entail assessment at only one level. Comprehension occurs at various levels-ranging from word, clause, sentence, paragraphs, and to a whole discourse (Voss et aI., 1982). Thus, immediate assessment would provide a limited view. Furthermore, Voss et a1. (1982) assert that comprehension of "a unit at least the size of a clause" requires remembrance of information that appeared earlier in the text and the integration of this information with subsequent information (p. 351). Accordingly, they conclude that comprehension requires the maintenance of information in short-term memory. They further point out that it would be difficult, and probably impossible to separate memory and comprehension because comprehension of larger units involves an inherent memory component.

Smith (1988) provides a thorough explication of the memory factors that are involved in reading to understand. Holding a similar view as Voss et aI., Smith construes reading comprehension as a dynamic inter-play of memory and comprehension. Specifically, Smith contends that there are three aspects of memory: (a) sensory store (b) short-term memory; and long-term memory. Sensory store relates to information that is first perceived by a "receptor organ" (such as the eye) and the brain (Smith, 1988, p. 88), for instance, the identification of letters or words. Short-term memory refers to the brief period that something holds our attention right after it is identified. An example of this, according to Smith, is the instance when we remember a telephone number as we are dialling it. The third aspect of memory, long-term memory, involves all that we know about the world, or prior knowledge.

Smith (1988) emphasizes that each aspect of memory has its limitations and its distinguishing characteristics. Short-term memory has limited capacity; it is very brief; its retrieval is immediate; and it is fast in terms of input. In contrast, long-term memory has an unlimited capacity and persistence; its retrieval is dependent on how information is organized upon reception; and its input is slow. Smith stresses that comprehension is important for the efficient organization of information in long-term memory. In addition, he points out that memorization (particularly rote memorization) interferes with comprehension because memorization monopolizes attention.

Thus, in remembering, we are not recalling verbatim, rather we reconstruct the meanings of what we have read. In summary, Smith (1988) views reading comprehension as involving different aspects of memory. Memory is part and parcel of the comprehension process. Likewise, Johnston (1983) considers memory and comprehension as interrelated. Studying one would necessitate the study of the other. Otherwise, according to Johnston (1983), it would be like "contemplating the sound of the proverbial tree falling in the primeval forest. It is philosophically interesting but practically and psychologically of minimal interest" (p. 18).

Eskey (1986) holds a similar view to that of Smith with regard to the kinds of memory involved in reading comprehension. Eskey reminds us that the limited capacity of human memory, and the limitation of knowledge of particular readers, are such that regardless of how intelligent a reader is, h/she will always be constrained in his or her reading by these limitations. The efficient reader therefore reads in the right proportion of "chunks" (reading in too small chunks will tax short-term memory), and learn to use the redundancy intrinsic in human languages together with knowledge of subject matter and knowledge of the world (Eskey, 1986,11).

COMPREHENSION: SUBSKILLS OR HOLISTIC SKILLS?

Whether comprehension is considered a holistic or a divisible process is another pertinent issue in a discussion of reading comprehension assessment. Is comprehension divided into separate subskills that can be identified and remedied for instruction? Or does comprehension involve a holistic process that cannot be broken down into distinct components? Alderson and Urquhart (1984) state that traditional approaches to reading comprehension have focused on the identification of a series of subskills. For instance, teachers are familiar with approaches that attempt to divide reading into skimming, scanning, identifying main ideas and details, reading for gist, and so forth. Studies of reading have attempted to discover the components of skills related to reading within taxonomies 0 r hierarchies of skills (Alderson & Urquhart, 1984). Grellet's (1981) book contains various exercises that are meant to teach reading via emphasis on the different reading skills.

Recent research, however, has been unsuccessful in providing evidence to support the existence of these separate skills (Alderson & Urquhart, 1984; Wallace, 1993). Researchers utilized various approaches to the study of separating these skills, from factor analysis to logical analysis (Johnston, 1983). Advocates of the holistic approach to reading have also provided empirical evidence to support their contentions. Thorndike (1974, cited in Johnston, 1983), considered the main proponent of the holistic view of reading comprehension, claims that reading is in fact reasoning; therefore it cannot be divided into distinct subprocesses. Johnston (1983) however, states that it would be advantageous to know a number of subskills in reading comprehension that can be subjected to remediation. This could serve as a useful framework that could guide assessment and changes in instruction. Alderson and Urquhart (1984) argue that the skills approach to reading comprehension assessment does not offer us any insights into how readers understand. The product of reading is different in terms of levels of meaning and comprehension, and comprehension does not reflect different skills. They further add that it is possible that different readers go through similar processes to arrive at different products.

Another limitation of the skills approach is the assumption that texts embody predictable meanings (Alderson & Urquhart, 1984). The belief is that all that the reader needs to do is to extract the meaning in the text if h/she is adequately skilful. A reader who has been taught the different skills such as grasping main ideas, understanding implied and stated information, understanding vocabulary in context, identifying affixes, and so forth, is supposed to be able to understand what the author is communicating through application of these skills. Assessment therefore is approached in terms of what the reader can demonstrate as a result of application of the skills taught (Myers, 1991). The debate on the process and product, as well as the subskills and holistic approaches of comprehension and its assessment has yet to be resolved. However, current theories and research on reading comprehension seem to point in the direction whereby reading comprehension is viewed as a constructive process. Several studies provide evidence in support of the centrality of the reader in reader-text interactions, and how different responses are reader-based rather than based on features of texts (Allen, Bernhardt, Berry, & Demel, 1988; Bernhardt, 1988; lee, 1986; Lee & Musumeci, 1988). Therefore, reader-based views of reading comprehension suggest that assessment of comprehension needs to include a reflection of the real reader, not a generic reader; describe adequately textual features; enable us to understand how and what readers utilize from texts for processing; and informs us of how culturally precise one can reconstruct a text (Bernhardt, 1988).

This view thus emphasizes a process approach. Johnston (1983) states that for diagnostic purposes, the problem remains that we have only product measures at hand, although our main interest is in process which is amenable to instructional change. She further adds that process and product should not be viewed as a dichotomy, but rather should be considered "complementary approaches to the same problem" (Johnston, 1983, 19).

CHAPTER 6

MEASURES OF COMPREHENSION

Assessments of reading comprehension are indirect measures; we can never truly capture the processes nor can we obtain a pure measure of how or what have been understood. Hence, all comprehension tests are merely "samples of indicators of 'real reading'" ... they are merely indices of the real thing, not the real thing itself." (Garcia & Pearson, 1991, 24). Despite being samples of behavior, the ubiquity of reading comprehension tests is suggestive of validity because many educators and the public have an unrelenting faith in their particular choice of tests (Farr & Carey, 1986). Thus, it is a common practice that outcomes of tests are used to provide information on one's ability to comprehend. In assessing reading comprehension, unfortunately, there appears to be a greater tendency towards the use of product measures over that of process measures. Consequently, many researchers and educators advocate the use of multiple measures of comprehension," and preferably the use of a combination of product and process measures or the use of a measure that closely reflect product and process (Aiken, 1987; Farr & Carey, 1986; Johnston, 1983; Shohamy, 1984; Spivey, 1989;Taylor, 1985; Garcia & Pearson, 1991; Seda, 1988; Myers, 1991; Pearson & Valencia, 1987; Winograd, Paris, & Bridge, 1991).

There are a variety of assessment approaches to comprehension in first language and second language contexts. Two common assessment approaches of reading comprehension are the written free recall task and multiple-choice questions. The following discussion is on these two measures of comprehension.

WRITTEN FREE- RECALL

The written free recall protocol has become an established measure of reading comprehension in L1 and L2 research (Refer to Chapter 7 for a description of the free recall). The consensus among researchers and educators in reading research and instruction is that the recall protocol is a construct valid and integrative instrument for the assessment of what students have understood after reading a text (Bernhardt, 1983, 1991; Wells, 1986; Berkemeyer, 1989; Hammadou, 1991; Smith & Jackson,

1985; Taylor, 1985; Irwin & Mitchell, 1983; Lee, 1986, 1990). Bernhardt (1983) and Johnston (1983), among others, state many advantages of using the recall protocol to assess comprehension. The recall protocol is considered the ... most straightforward assessment ... of the result of the text-reader interaction "(Johnston, 1983, 54) and one that "circumvents the pitfalls of traditional test design and, at the same time, focuses on the communication between text and reader." (Bernhardt, 1983, 28). The written free recall protocol reflects assessment that is in line with the current view of comprehension as an interactive, constructive process (Bernhardt, 1991; Kamil, 1986; Spiro, 1980; Spivey, 1989).

Numerous L1 and L2 studies on reading comprehension have shown that free recall provides a wealth of information not only on the content of texts read, but also on how meaning is reconstructed (Clark, 1982; Taylor, 1980, 1985; Smith & Jackson, 1985; Pollack, 1990; Davey, 1989; Connor, 1984; Lee, 1990; Carrell, 1983; Frary, 1985). Bernhardt (1991) states that the use of written recall in second language studies is not something new for it has been used as a dependent measure in several research studies beginning in the 1970s. Some of these studies that used the written recall protocols are cited in her book *Reading Development in a Second Language.* Among some of the advantages of the written free recall technique as outlined by Bernhardt (1983) are: (a) students are unable to guess their way through texts, (b) the technique does not impede students' understanding of the text, (c) it provides quantitative as well as qualitative data on what readers have comprehended, (d) although it does not test grammar, it does reveal weaknesses in grammar that interfere with readers' text interaction, (e) it stresses the importance of comprehending the text read, (f) it induces positive feelings because readers are not penalized for paraphrases, (g) it is able to tap or reveal individual comprehension strategies, (h) it provides the teacher with an opportunity to customize instruction to individual needs, and (i) it is relatively easy for the teacher to prepare in terms of texts to be read.

Bernhardt (1983, 1986, 1990), and in collaboration with other researchers (Bernhardt & Berkemeyer, 1988; Bernhardt & James, 1987; Allen, Bernhardt, Berry, & Demel, 1988) conducted a number of studies using the written recall protocol to assess reading comprehension of second language and foreign language learners of German, Spanish, and French. In all these studies it was found that students' recalls provide rich information on "the organization of the stored information" (Johnston, 1983, 54). Bernhardt (1986) asserts that the recall protocols provide the teacher with a sense of what real readers do with real texts. In instruction, teachers are able to "teach from learners rather than at them."(p.108).

There are some caveats that should be considered in the use of the written recall protocol for both research and classroom use. Johnston (1983) points out that although much can be inferred from and about what is recalled, nothing can be said about the understanding and memory of what is not recalled. In addition, he states that the cognitive demand of the recall task in the form of the large memory component and possible retrieval problems require that the readers fully understand the requirements in performing the task. For instance, readers must be aware of the kinds of information that they need to produce, the level of details, and the extent to which recall should maintain the surface structure of the passage read.

Another limitation of the recall protocol is its reliance on the need for production skills. For example, in written recall, the reader must be fairly skilled in writing, but most teachers are aware that production skills differ across readers. This is a problem in assessing readers of a second or foreign language whose production abilities in the second or foreign language are weak; they may be able to understand what they read, but may have production problems due to low language proficiency. A solution to this, that has been adopted by some researchers in reading research, is the use of recalls written in the language the readers are proficient in or in readers' native language (Bernhardt, 1983; Bernhardt & Berkemeyer, 1988; Demel, 1990; Hammadou, 1991; Lee, 1986,1990; Lee & Ballman, 1987; Lee & Riley, 1990;Wolff, 1987). In this way, students' reproductive skills will not interfere with their abilities to comprehend (Bernhardt & James, 1987).

It is apparent that the written recall protocol is a widely used instrument in the assessment of reading comprehension. A majority of recent studies in reading in a native language have either used the written recall as a dependent measure or in combination with other measures (e.g., Amlund, Kardash, & Kulhavy, 1986; Kincade, 1991; Meyer & Freedle,1984; Yochum, 1991). For instance, Taylor (1985) examined the use of various measures of recall to assess comprehension of expository text. She conducted an informal survey of the major research journals, such as the *Journal of Reading Behavior and Reading Research Quarterly,* and found that out of fifteen journals that dealt with expository text, half used some kind of recall measure. And a majority of these studies used a written recall over oral recall. Taylor suggests that a free recall maybe a more sensitive measure of comprehension than other commonly used techniques. Question-answering entails a focus on only the number of questions answered correctly. However, based on a study by Taylor, she concludes that within the recall approach itself, the summary forms a better measure of comprehension than the free recall. The free recall requires that readers recall everything they remember, whereas in performing a summary, readers form a gist of what is read rather than producing everything found in the text (Kintsch & van Dijk, 1978).

Research in second language and foreign language reading is also replete with studies that employ the use of the written recall to assess comprehension. Lee (1986) reviewed a number of studies in second language reading in which the free written recall task was used as a dependent measure. The studies he examined were that of Bernhardt (1983), Carrell (1983, 1984a, & 1984b), and Connor (1984), and he found variations in design and findings. He noted that Bernhardt (1983) asked their subjects to recall in their native language, whereas all of Carrell's studies and Connor's study had the subjects recall in their second language. The justification for the use of the native language as the language of recall was the assumption that this would avoid the problem of limited second language production abilities.

Lee noted further that the conditions under which the tasks were administered were also different for different studies. Most of the studies used an immediate written recall task; however, only Carrell's (1984a, 1984b) two studies used a delayed recall task. In addition, Carrell (1984b) did not orient the students towards reading for the purpose of recalling the information read. Based on his review of studies that employed written recalls, Lee (1986) conducted a study to investigate whether there would be differences between planned versus unplanned recall, and whether the language of response (recall) made a difference (i.e., L1 vs. L2 recall). Lee was interested in the quantity of recalled information under the two conditions of recall. The free written recall was used as a dependent measure.

In the study, Lee (1986) had 320 students from four different semester-level Spanish classes at the Michigan State University and at the University of Michigan read either a passage with prereading instructions or one without the prereading instructions. All the oral and written directions were in English, the native language of the subjects. At each semester level, students were divided into two groups. One group recalled in English (L1) and the other group recalled in Spanish (L2). In addition, per semester level, a group of students read the passage without prereading instructions, whereas the other group read the passage with prereading instructions. Thus, there were four groups with four levels per group. Each group of the sixteen groups comprised 20 students. The passage was divided into idea units, which served as a scoring template. The written recall protocols were scored by two raters for number of idea units that each protocol contained, and then it was compared to the template to find out the number of idea units that corresponded to the idea units in the scoring template. A three-way ANOVA or analysis of variance was used to analyze the data.

The results indicated main effects for language of recall and level of learner. Students who wrote in their native language (L1) recalled more information than those who had recalled in their second language (L2). Lee also found that there was no interaction between level and language of recall. However, there was an interaction between directions (pre- reading vs. no prereading) and level of learners. Based on his study and those studies he reviewed, Lee concluded that recall can be affected by the conditions under which it is administered. Recalling in a native language seems to provide more information than recalling in a second language. He further asserted that studies that employ only one level of learners (e.g., elementary or advanced) are of limited generalizibility. He cited Hudson's (1982) study that found differential effects of methods of improving comprehension based on level of learner. Lee suggests the use of several levels of learners of different proficiencies to enable comparison across levels.

Another study that used the written recall approach is that of Bernhardt (1983). This study provided empirical evidence that supports the interactive nature of reading that involves multisources of factors- text based and reader-based. In her study, the students were asked to read a passage silently as many times as they desired. Once they felt certain they had understood the text, they surrendered the passage to the instructor. Next, they were instructed to write down everything they could remember from the passage. The students were told to write in English, their native language. The instrument against which the recalls were scored was developed by "slashing prose into meaningful segments" (Bernhardt, 1983, p. 29). The meaningful idea units consisted of mainly nouns, verbs, and prepositional phrases. The interrater reliability was reported as .83 (Bernhardt, 1983, p. 29). Each idea unit was awarded one point. Analyses of the recall protocol revealed not only what was reconstructed, but also how meaning was reconstructed. Each of the students' recall protocols demonstrates various differing information based on individual reader factors. For example, one student showed comprehension of a large percentage of the text's content- mentioning the major points; provided a grasp of the meaning of the text; and provided a coherent reconstruction of the text read. Another student missed much of the major points, and provided an illogical conclusion.

Bernhardt (1983) emphasizes the significance of reader affect in the study. Students were instructed to reconstruct their understanding of the text in English; this could lead to positive feelings since the students are not penalized for writing or paraphrasing in incorrect German. However, according to Bernhardt, writing in the native language may have a negative effect in terms of motivation to learn the second language vocabulary and structures. Nevertheless, in her other studies and writings, since then, Bernhardt (1985, 1987, 1988, 1991) has successfully been able to provide convincing evidence to support the use of the written recall protocol as an assessment instrument of reading comprehension in the area of second language reading. Bernhardt's 1985 study on learners of German reading a German literary text is another study that serves to provide empirical and theoretical evidence of the validity of written recall protocol to assess comprehension. In this study, she maintained that research on constructive processes in comprehension is a "burgeoning line of research in the United States.", and she suggested the need for cross-national studies to be conducted to "investigate truly the L2 comprehension process" (Bernhardt, 1985,42).

One such cross-cultural study that had used the written recall protocol was that conducted by Steffensen, Joag-dev, and Anderson (1979). However, this study was conducted in the United States where the foreign subjects were constantly exposed to the language they were learning and to American culture. In their study, the researchers found that subjects read the text from their native culture with greater facility, recalled more information, produced more culturally appropriate elaborations, than when they read the text from the foreign culture. In addition, they found that the students produced more culturally based distortions of the foreign passage (Steffensen et aI., 1979, 10).

The texts were about an Indian (from India) wedding and an American wedding. Subjects were told to read their own native passage and the foreign passage. They then produced a written recall in English. The results of the study were found to be consistent with schematheory. This study was an investigation into the effects of culture-specific knowledge, and the dependent measure used was the immediate written recall.

Various other studies in Ll and L2 reading have used the written recall protocol to investigate effects of independent variables on the recall scores, or differences in recall between native and non-native readers or between poor and good readers (e.g., Connor, 1984; Wells, 1986; Mandler, Scribner, Cole, & DeForest, 1980; Carrell & Floyd, 1987; Hague, 1989; Lee & Riley, 1990; Demel, 1990; Hammadou, 1991;1ohnson, 1981; among others).

SCORING RECALL PROTOCOLS

The biggest problem of using written recall protocols has been the lack of a valid scoring system (Wells, 1986; Pollack, 1990; Clark, 1982). Voss et al. (1982) point out that the necessity to score recall protocols has led researchers to divide texts into units. A technique often used is to divide a passage into "idea units" or "units of text that embody a single complete idea." (Voss et aI., 1982,352). These idea units form the template for scoring protocols. The particular idea unit and the number of idea units recalled in the subject's recall protocol are then compared to the idea units in the scoring template. A limitation of scoring in idea units is that whereas it allows for quantification of the amount of idea units recalled, it does not provide for qualitative differences (Voss et aI., 1982).

Another system of dividing text is Johnson's (1970) "pausal acceptability units." These units are developed by asking subjects to indicate where pausing occurs. That is, pausing as one reads the passage orally to "catch a breath, to give emphasis to the story, or to enhance meaning" (Johnson, 1970, 13). In addition, the units that have been segmented are rated according to their importance to the text as a whole. This permits a researcher to make qualitative distinctions since the pausal units are assigned different values (given weights) in accordance to its relative importance to the passage. Johnson does this by deleting units until one-fourth, one-half, or three-fourths of the original words of the text are left. Johnson (1973) also related pausal units to meaningfulness. The pausal unit method has been used to study developmental changes in metacognitive abilities of children (Brown & Smiley, 1977; Petros & Hoving, 1980; cited in Voss et aI., 1982). Examples of studies of reading in L1 and L2 that utilized text segmentation by pausal units are those of Bernhardt (1988, 1991), Clark (1982), Hammadou (1991), and Lee and Ballman (1987).

Bernhardt (1991) states that the pausal units form a simple propositional analysis system, and the propositions can be weighted by having raters rank each pausal unit in terms of its salience to the text. Bernhardt (1991) used student protocols in a study by Allen, Bernhardt, Berry, and Demel (1988) to compare the pausal units system with that of Meyer's (1985) recall protocol system. Using the text from the Allen et al. study, Bernhardt had three fluent readers of German read each text (two were used) to themselves and to put a slash at every point that they paused. She points out that in most L1 research, pausal endings are generally found at ends of a syntactically related unit. The pausal acceptability units totalled 127 propositions compared to Meyer's system which yielded 160 lines of text (Bernhardt, 1991, 209).

The pausal units were weighted according to Johnson's (1970) method. That is, the text is first divided into pausal units. Two fluent readers were asked to segment the text into four levels: the lowest level is the least important 25 percent of the units in the text, the next Ievel is the next least important 25 percent, and so forth. Values from 1 to 4 are assigned to the pausal units in terms of importance. For instance, the lowest 25 percent is given the value 1, and the highest or the most salient information is given a value 4. A high correlation between this scoring system and Meyer's system was achieved (Bernhardt, 1991, p. 209). Bernhardt concludes that there is sufficient overlap in the scores to suggest that both systems are tapping the same behavior. She therefore argues that the more efficient system (pausal units) is the better. Bernhardt claims that scoring of the weighted or unweighted protocols utilized approximately ten minutes. In addition, Bernhardt suggests that this system can be used on the computer via the use of spread sheets that could do sorting and calculations of information in the propositions. Therefore, the advantage of the pausal unit system is that it is efficient to use (especially on computer) and when used in a recall protocol provides rich qualitative information.

The scoring system commonly used for recall protocols in L1 and L2 research studies on reading has been Meyer's (1985) method. Meyer's system for scoring recall protocols was derived from her study on how and why certain ideas are better recalled from a passage. Consequently, based on her study she produced her book *The Organization of Prose and its Effects on Memory.* Meyer's system is based on Grice's (1975, cited in Meyer, 1975) case grammar. This system identifies the structural characteristics and lexical units of a text in a hierarchical arrangement (Bernhardt, 1991). This way, the system shows the particular lexical and relational units that are recalled, including its position in the structure of the text. Bernhardt (1991) provides a clear explication of how the recall protocol scoring template following Meyer's system is developed. A complete description of the system can be found in Meyer's 1975 book (23-53).

There are a plethora of studies in L1 reading that used Meyer's system of text analysis and scoring, studies in L2 reading comprehension that used Meyer's system include that of Connor (1984), Allen et al. (1988), Bernhardt and Berkemeyer (1988), Demel (1990), Hague (1989), and Wells (1986). Although Meyer's system is considered valid and reliable in analyzing recall protocols (Wells, 1986), there are certain disadvantages of the method. Bernhardt (1991) points to two of its weaknesses: (a) developing a scoring template from the text hierarchy requires a large amount of time, that is, between 25 to 50 hours for each 250-word text, and (b) the amount of time needed to score the presence or absence of relationships within the text structure requires approximately 30 minutes to one hour to score each student's protocol (pp. 202-203). Other scoring systems are in the form of propositional idea units (Bransford & Johnson, 1973; Turner & Greene, 1977, cited in

Wolff, 1987), or in the form of either rating sheets (Smith & Jackson, 1985) or checklists of holistic scoring (Irwin & Mitchell, 1983; Taylor, 1985).

MULTIPLE·CHOICE QUESTIONS

The multiple-choice test is historically and presently the most common form of comprehension assessment in education (Aiken, 1987; Farr & Carey, 1986; Parr, Pritchard, & Smitten, 1990; Statman, 1988; Wesdorp, 1983; Perkins & Parish, 1988; Johnston, 1983). It is also considered to be probably "the most researched, most maligned, most difficult to construct, most abused, yet most functional of all items (when properly harnessed)" (Johnston, 1983, 59). The typical format comes in the form of a short passage accompanied by several multiple-choice questions with a single predetermined correct answer. Although a popular approach to assessing comprehension, multiple-choice question measures have both advantages and limitations. Over the past decades, numerous studies have been conducted on multiple-choice tests, and the literature on reading comprehension in L1 and L2 contain an immense number of citation of studies that either used the multiple-choice format alone, or in combination with some other test formats (Starman, 1988). Consequently, there are various concerns over its relative merits and limitations that have sparked ongoing debates. Nevertheless, in spite of controversy, multiple-choice tests continue to proliferate (Farr & Carey, 1986).

Aiken (1987) states several advantages of multiple-choice questions: (a) the multiple-choice items are more reliable than other test items due to their objectivity and their ability to be less susceptible to effects of guessing (compared to true/false items); (b) multiplechoice question tests are versatile in terms of ability to measure specific and complex objectives at nearly all levels of proficiency and domains; (c) multiple- choice questions provide an adequate sampling of the domains to be tested; (d) multiple-choice items can be quickly and accurately scored; (e) multiple-choice items enable easy and objective item analysis; and (f) multiple-choice tests provide diagnostic information through analyses of responses to the alternatives in the items (p. 4).

Johnston (1983) argues that multiple-choice questions, other than serving as a means of large-scale objective scoring and reduction in chance score from that of true/false questions, provide similar information to that of true/false items. That is, multiple-choice and true/false items merely provide right versus wrong answers, thus what is reduced is only the "noise" factor (Johnston, 1983, 59). However, Johnston maintains that with a theory-driven procedure, the multiple-choice questions may be able to give us more information. The main attraction of multiple-choice questions is in their perceived ability to produce a ... clean, neat, scientific score ... (Farr & Carey, 1986, 34). As such, this efficiency and objectivity has turned multiple-choice tests into the most economical technique of determining the extent to which schools are successful in doing their jobs (Farr & Carey, 1986).

Likewise, Oller (1979) contends that the popularity of multiple-choice tests are due to their presumed objectivity and reliability of scoring. Furthermore, he states that multiple-choice tests are economical in terms of the required effort and expense for its administration, and this is true only if the multiple-choice tests are valid and reliable in the first place. However, Oller argues that multiple-choice tests may not necessarily be any more reliable and valid than tests of different formats, for in some instances, open-ended formats tend to be more reliable and valid. In addition, although Oller acknowledges the administrative and scoring convenience of multiple-choice tests, he cautions anyone against the practice of including multiple-choice tests, as part of daily classroom instruction. He asserts that it is mainly a matter of practicality that many choose to use the multiple-choice questions, and that this decision is not related to reliability and validity in the general sense of these terms.

Serious problems are associated with multiple-choice questions. Many researchers and educators (e.g., Aiken, 1987; Badger, 1990; Bernhardt, 1991; Perkins, 1984; Perkins & Parish, 1988; Johnston, 1983, 1984; Oller, 1979; Pyrczak, 1975; Statman, 1979) point to the following problems of multiple-choice questions that pose limitations in their use as a comprehension assessment technique:

1. The insistence on a single correct answer is a major problem. Current research views of reading emphasize the constructive nature of reading comprehension whereby understanding involves not only features of text, but also features within the reader such as back- ground knowledge, attitude, and so forth.

2. The form of multiple-choice questions is at odds with advances in theory of cognition, learning, and language learning. Using multiple- choice questions suggests acceptance of certain theoretical assumptions regarding learning, how we remember information, how learning is measured, how we read, and how language is measured. These are questions basic to education. Research has shown that different readers interpret the same texts differently due to the influence of the individual reader's prior knowledge. Insisting on one correct answer is counter to the theory of how people read and comprehend texts; comprehension cannot be defined as word-based or unidimensional (Oller, 1979).

3. Good items are difficult to construct. There are more ways of violating the principles of writing good items than there are in writing them (Oller, 1979). Items must be evaluated for content, clarity of wordings, and balance among the alternatives. Items assessing higher-order objectives are difficult to construct, and to ensure parallel alternatives as choices.

4. Multiple-choice items require a longer response time. Consequently, the time constraint results in an inadequate sampling of subject matter.

5. The emphasis in multiple-choice questions is on recognition of the predetermined correct answer rather than on recall and organization of information read. Interest is on the answer, not on the quality of thinking underlying the answer or the skill used to express it.

6. Multiple-choice items favor the "shrewd, nimblewitted, rapid reader" (Aiken, 1987,44), but penalize the creative reader who is capable of going beyond the conventional, expected response due to the reader's particular prior knowledge (Aiken, 1987; Bernhardt, 1983; Farr & Carey, 1986; Perkins & Parish, 1988; Spivey, 1989).

7. A multiple-choice question format has negative socioeducational effects. Scores on multiple-choice question examinations (e.g., standardized tests) are weak measures of overall ability and achievement. The use of only multiple-choice questions in examinations encourages inferior instruction and bad study habits (Aiken, 1987). Negative back- wash effects are also associated with multiple-choice tests (Wesdorp, 1983); for example, the assumption of many critics about multiple- choice tests is that students who are exposed throughout their education to tests and instructions using multiple-choice questions become weak in production skills, especially in their writing skills.

Some teachers of reading tend to teach to the test, and thus ignore the importance of facilitating students' meaning construction when students read texts. The focus is on how to get the right answer through using cues in the passage and in the items of the multiple- choice format. In the discussion of multiple-choice questions, inevitably various issues are raised. In a critical review of research conducted over the past two decades on multiple-choice questions, Aiken (1987) raised some of these issues that include item construction (e.g., number of options; complex items; and item arrangement), announced versus unannounced multiple-choice tests, problems of guessing, strategies of answering test items, and item analysis. More recent investigations of multiple-choice tests attempt to show how this type of assessment can be used effectively to measure reading comprehension (Farr, Pritchard, & Smitten, 1990;Jorcey, 1987; Statman, 1988; Wixson & Peters, 1987).

Farr, Pritchard, and Smitten (1990) investigated the comprehension strategies of a group of native English speaking college students on a multiple-choice task. Subjects were randomly assigned to either an introspective interview method, where they had first to report on-line what they were reading and thinking as they read the test passage, and then answered the multiple-choice questions, or to a retrospective interview method where they had to read the passage first, uninterrupted, do the multiple-choice questions, and then recount to the researcher how they had read and comprehended. It was found that the subjects' approach to the multiple-choice test was to focus on the questions as quickly as possible, and then using the questions to guide the search in the passage for the best answer to the multiple-choice questions. Thus, the students did not first read and understand the passage and later turn to the questions, instead they treated the questions and the passage as a whole interrelated task. The subjects were more interested in getting the right answers than on understanding the content of the passage. The study suggests that multiple-choice tests are valid as one type of reading; that is, reading to answer questions (Farr et al., 1990). The researchers contend that because multiple-choice reading comprehension tests- require strategies of searching for answers, this activity can be considered a sensible estimate of overall reading ability. Farr et al. (1990) believe that this study supports the construct validity of multiple-choice reading comprehension tests, for at least this particular type of reading task.

The construction of a multiple-choice test from an interactive view of reading was examined by Wixson and Peters (1987). The rationale for using a multiple-choice format was the concern over the confounding effect of using alternative formats; students are more familiar with the multiple-choice test than other forms. The researchers claim that the multiple-choice questions that were used required complex reasoning because the distractors used provide accurate information or inferences from the passage, but are incorrect answers to the questions (except for one appropriate answer to the question). Item generation in the study reflected a constructive, integrative process of comprehension. The implication of the study is that the multiple-choice testing method can be constructed in a way that is consistent with current theories of reading comprehension.

Another long-debated issue of multiple-choice questions concerns the passage dependency or independency of questions. Pyrczak (1975) conducted a study on multiple-choice questions and found that there was no difference between students who read the test passage and chose an answer from the alternatives, and those students who merely selected an answer from the alternatives without having read the passage. Pyrczak attributed this result to such factors as: (a) students' prior knowledge, (b) the nature of constructing multiple-choice questions as a whole, and (c) the interrelatedness of the questions. Passage dependent questions are important, otherwise students will not have to read the passage closely, or do not have to read the passage at all; this would defeat the purpose of reading instruction (Pyrczak & Axelrod, 1976).

Multiple-choice tests in a second or foreign language situation can pose a problem because teachers do not have much choice in using synonyms, for students often have limited vocabularies (Bernhardt, 1991). As a result, teachers are driven into repeating parts of the passage which in turn will reduce the test into "a word recognition and matching exercise" (Bernhardt, 1991, 199). This problem is illustrated in Hosenfeld's (1977, cited in Bernhardt, 1991) study on reading/ grammar tasks. Students in the study focussed on grammatical cues and used these cues to perform grammatical manipulations, instead of reading for the information in the passage.

Despite the various limitations of the multiple-choice format, multiple- choice questions remain widely used today. Many educators and researchers have accepted the fact that the multiple-choice questions task has many problems, but because of its objectivity and ease of administration and scoring, these educators and researchers are willing to overlook the shortcomings of the multiple-choice format in assessing comprehension. In dealing with the drawbacks of the multiple-choice testing method, various attempts have been made in research to improve on item construction (e.g., Statman, 1988; Perkins, 1984), and to teach students strategies of taking multiple-choice tests (e.g. Jorcey, 1987).

In testing reading comprehension in a second or foreign language, the attempt has also been to introduce the language of response or the language of the items in the multiple-choice test in the native or first language of the examinees (e.g., Lutjeharrns, 1986; Shohamy, 1984; Tan & Ling, 1979; Wolf, 1991). Tan and Ling (1979) for instance, found that multiple-choice items written in the native language, *Bahasa Malaysia,* had a facilitative effect on their subjects' performance. The students had less chances of misinterpreting the question stems, and also, it is advantageous effectively for the students to answer questions in a language with which they are familiar, especially under the conditions of a testing situation. Although the passage was in English, answering multiple-choice questions in the native language resulted in higher scores for these students.

COMPARATIVE STUDIES OFTESTING METHODS OR TASKS

One of the research questions that was posited in this study was whether there are any quantitative differences between student's performance on the two testing methods or tasks, the immediate written recall and the multiple-choice question task, as revealed by students' reading comprehension scores on the same reading passage. Research studies on testing methods include that of Badger (1990), Bender (1980), Davey (1989), Head, Readence, & Buss (1989), Lutjeharms (1982, 1986), Samson (1983), Seda (1988), Shohamy (1984), Stathman (1979), and Wolf (1991). The researchers examined whether different testing methods or tasks had any effect on the subjects' scores on reading comprehension tests.

Badger (1990) conducted a study testing the comprehension of twelfth-grade students in the area of Science and Mathematics using multiple-choice questions and open-ended questions. All students had to perform on both types of testing. The scores on the multiple-choice and open-ended question tasks were compared, and it was found that the correlation obtained was moderately high. Besides that, it was found that the open-ended questions provided more direct evidence of students' understanding than the multiple-choice task. Further, upon analyses of the responses on the open-ended task, it was found that this type of questions possess the potential as instructional devices. Badger states that because the multiple-choice items are constructed to produce a single correct answer, they are not conducive to examinations or discussions that could promote learning. On the contrary, the open-ended or free response items lead to a wider range of acceptable answers and strategies, in addition to providing practical evidence of misunderstandings and faulty reasoning (Badger, 1990, 14).

Samson (1983) conducted a similar study to that of Badger's study.However, in Samson's study she included another testing method, summary writing, and compared this to the other two methods (multiple- choice and open-ended questions). Samson reported no main differences among the three testing methods of assessing comprehension, and consequently concluded that the three methods measure the same trait, that is, comprehension. She found that among the three methods, the multiple-choice task was the easiest, next was the open- ended task, and finally the summary task. However, Shohamy (1984) criticized the study, pointing to its weak design. The same students had to perform on all three testing methods and to read the same passage thrice. Hence, there was a possibility of a practice effect and order of task effect (the tasks were not counterbalanced in terms of order of presentation).

Bender (1980) studied the kinds of strategies that readers use in performing two different types of testing methods on a reading comprehension task. Specifically, he examined the kinds of cues that readers use in retrieving information. He found that the selection strategy is the optimal strategy used for processing multiple-choice questions. The free recall (open-ended questions) requires specific cues rather than general context cues. In addition, Bender found that specific cues are facilitative for multiple-choice questions if they are in the alternatives rather than in the stems. The study points to the differences in the processing of multiple-choice and open-ended questions. Because the free recall or open-ended task typically provides the least cue information, it thus provides the lowest recall levels for specific information in the text read (Schuster & Crouse, 1972, cited in Bender, 1980).

Other similar studies comparing the multiple-choice questions and open-ended questions were conducted by Davey (1989), Lutjeharms (1982, 1986), Shohamy (1984), and Wolf (1991). Davey (1989) conducted a number of studies over a five-year period on various variables of question types that could affect reading comprehension. One such variable she examined was the effect of question format on readers' comprehension performance. The results of several of her studies indicated that multiple-choice question scores were generally higher than that of free response scores for all the subjects in the study. Further, it was found that questions requiring written responses are difficult for different readers. Poor readers had performed comparably to good readers on the multiple-choice task, but did much worse on the free response items.

Lutjeharms (1982, 1986) compared the responses of Dutch students reading German texts on multiple-choice and open-ended questions. The questions were written in students' native language (Dutch). The results indicate that the open-ended questions discriminated better than the multiple-question task. Similarly, Shohamy (1984) found that performance of her subjects on a multiple-choice question test was better than for those subjects who sat for either the open-minded question test or the cloze test. It was also evident that questions posed in the native language of the subjects (Hebrew) proved to be more facilitative of comprehension than when the questions were worded in the target language (English). The results of the study indicate that the multiple- choice is the easier task compared to the open-ended questions, and the open-ended questions are in turn, easier than the cloze task.

Wolf's (1991) findings on the effect of differences in testing methods or tasks on students' comprehension scores are similar to that of Shohamy's (1984) findings. Wolf found significant effects for type of task-multiple-choice, open-ended, and cloze and language of response (native language vs. foreign language). The three tasks were constructed in a Spanish version (target language) and in an English version (native language of subjects). The subjects (N= 144) were from two levels of Spanish as a foreign language class (advanced and fourth semester learners). Wolf also found that the advanced students outperformed the fourth semester learners.

Another study that compared two different methods of testing reading comprehension is that of Head, Readence, and Buss (1989). Head et. al. investigated the effects of topic familiarity, writing ability, and summarization training on seventh-grade subjects reading a social studies text. Correlational analyses were used to examine any relationship between multiple-choice questions and summary scores. The results indicate that multiple-choice questions and summaries share very little overlap in the types of comprehension the two tasks assessed. The researchers concluded that because different methods of comprehension tap different behaviors, it is recommended that in assessing reading comprehension, multiple measures should be used.

A study that examined the validity of different testing methods was conducted by Seda (1988). Seda compared two different types of multiple-choice tests (traditional MC and a novel MC with multiple plausible answers per question) with two free-response measures (verbal retellings and semi-structured interviews). The qualitative analyses indicated that performance was different for different assessment approaches. She concluded that different testing formats thus tap different processes, or different parts of a single process (Seda, 1988, 3).

Stathman (1979) similarly found that different testing methods seem to reveal different information regarding readers' understandings. In a final examination paper for students of English as a foreign language, she included multiple-choice questions and short-answer questions (equal proportions of items from each type of testing method). The results indicated that seventy-five percent of the students had the same number of correct answers on both the multiple-choice and short-answer questions. Twenty percent of students scored higher on the short-answer than on the multiple-choice task. In addition, the students found the variety in test format interesting and thus motivating. Stathman recommends the use of both measures of comprehension instead of the sole dependence on a single method of testing such as multiple-choice questions.

The central focus of several comparative studies of testing methods conducted in the area of L1 and L2 reading comprehension has been on the comparison between common measures of comprehension such as multiple-choice questions, open-ended questions, short-answer questions, cloze, and until recently, written summaries. Studies that utilized the written recall (recall everything understood and remembered) had used the written recall as a dependent measure.

CHAPTER 7

COMPARING TWO TASKS: WRITTEN-RECALL AND MULTIPLE CHOICE QUESTIONS

Maarof (1993) conducted a study to investigate the kinds of information that two testing methods or tasks of reading comprehension of an expository text may yield. The two testing methods compared were the Immediate Written Recall (IWR) task and the Multiple-Choice (MC) task. Specifically, the study was an investigation into the effects of type of task on Malaysian ESL university students' reading comprehension scores. In addition, the effect of proficiency level was investigated, as well as any interactions of task and proficiency level. The study also examined whether a sample of students' recall protocols could be analyzed and categorized using Bernhardt's (1983) *Constructivist Model of Second Language Reading.* Performance of students on the two tasks for each proficiency level was examined and the scores were compared to see whether there were significant differences. This chapter describes how the study was conducted and includes findings of the study.

SUBJECTS

A total number of 180 subjects were randomly selected to participate in the study. Subjects were drawn from three ethnic groups: Malay, Chinese, and Indian. Subjects from both sexes were included. The subjects were between 19 and 40 years old. The average age of the sample of subjects was 22 years old. The subjects were drawn from the three levels of reading proficiency courses in the Department of English Language, National University of Malaysia. The three levels of reading courses were: (a) VEI003, Reading for General Purposes; (b) VE1043, Reading Skills; and (c) VE1053, Academic Reading.

Level of proficiency as was used in the study refers to these three levels of reading courses. Students were initially placed into these three levels of reading courses based on their performance in the "English Language Proficiency Test" (ELPT) of the Language Center at the university.

For the study, including students from the three levels of courses or of English language proficiency was an attempt to avoid an overly homogenous sampling that could affect reliability and variance for analysis (Hatch & Lazarathon, 1991). The population of interest was restricted to the students in the three levels of reading courses. Further, only the afternoon sections of these courses were included in the study. A random sampling of all students in all three levels of the reading proficiency courses did not seem feasible. Instead, a random sampling procedure was used to draw subjects from each of the three levels of reading courses in the afternoon sections (n = 60 per course). Within each course, students were then randomly assigned (using a table of random numbers) to either one of the two testing methods (IWR or MC).

RESEARCH SETTING

The experimental test took place on the university's campus, and was conducted at the university's main hall or *Dewan Besar.* Subjects were informed through their respective course instructors that they had been selected at random to participate in a study. The subjects were informed of the purpose of the study; that is, an attempt to understand what students do when they read for understanding in English, and whether the specific type of task assessing comprehension could affect their performance.

SAMPLING

Subjects were drawn from the three levels of reading courses. This type of sampling is referred to as a stratified random sampling procedure (Brown, 1988; Brewer, 1984, 1989). In other words, the subjects were blocked by reading proficiency level. In addition, within each level of course, students were randomly assigned to either the IWR task or the MC task.

A minimum sample size was determined through power analysis following Cohen's (1988) procedure. The alpha level was set at alpha = .05, beta = .20, and effect size at E.S. = .25. A medium effect size was chosen and a bidirectional test was adopted in the light of the knowledge that no similar studies have previously been conducted. Furthermore, a medium effect size seemed most practically significant. Based upon Cohen's power tables (1988, 384-385) for analysis of variance, cell sample sizes were determined for each main effect of task and proficiency level and for any interactions of these factors. Hence, the largest sample size needed to test for any effects and interactions was found to be N = 162. However, a slightly bigger sample size of N = 180 was drawn from the population of interest to control for attrition of subjects.

INSTRUMENTS

All subjects read a 306-words expository passage about the story of "Thanksgiving Day" in America. Then, subjects either performed on an immediate written recall task or a multiple-choice task, depending upon which task the students had been earlier assigned to.

TEST PASSAGE

The passage selected that was considered appropriate for the subjects was an expository, descriptive passage entitled "The Story of Thanksgiving" from the book *Ready to Read* by Ruth Brancard and Jeanne Hind. The book is designed for "adult and young adult learners of English as a second language." (Brancard & Hind, 1989, xi). The passage was modified to a length of 306 words. The modification was conducted not for the purpose of simplification, rather it was to reduce the length of the text. The resulting slightly shortened text (from the original 455 words to a shortened version of 306 words) was reproduced on an 8 x 111/2 paper, and copies were made for each subject. The passage's title was omitted to increase the difficulty level of the passage, and to make the reading text a more challenging task for the subjects. The criteria used for selection of the passage are as follows:

1. An expository text was chosen in light of the widely-held view that expository texts represent the genre of discourse that students of ESL (Eskey, 1986; Powell, 1988), and particularly students at the National University of Malaysia, often deal with in their academic studies.
2. The text chosen is factual and informative. It is of the descriptive type; and thus is said to be less facilitative to recall (Meyer & Freedle, 1984). However, it was considered appropriate as a test passage so that difficulties that may arise as a result of students' interactions with the text could surface, and hence help reveal the kinds of problems or miscomprehensions students encounter in reading the text.
3. The content of the passage is culture specific-to American culture-s- however, it is sufficiently general in that it deals with traditional holidays and festivities. Students are familiar with holidays and festivals in Malaysia, and because holidays in general share certain universal elements, it was assumed that students would not find the overall passage content to be very alien. The particular topic "Thanksgiving Day" was also chosen so that it would not bias any student in terms of overall prior knowledge, because the topic is a typical American holiday. The issue of prior knowledge of the topic was dealt with in the study by including a "topic familiarity" task.
4. The topic is interesting enough so as to motivate students to read for understanding. Furthermore, the passage deals with an authentic topic drawn from real-life events.

READABILITY OF TEST-PASSAGE

The passage chosen for the study was estimated for its readability difficulty by means of the computer software *The Readability Machine* (Pasch, 1986). This program provides readability estimates using eight well-known and reliable formulae. A study by Hamsik (1984) indicates that readability formulae developed to assess reading difficulty for native English readers can be used with ESL students in the selection of appropriate reading materials.

Current research in reading questions the use of readability formulae because the ease or difficulty of texts is not dependent upon features of texts alone. However, the use of readability formulae together with subjective judgements of the teacher or researcher can assist in the selection of materials for the appropriate audience and purpose (Fry, 1990). The overall average readability level of the "Thanksgiving" passage was found to be at the eighth-grade level. This was considered to be at a slightly difficult level for the subjects, and thus deemed appropriate for the purpose of the study. A slightly difficult passage would serve as a challenge for the subjects, in addition to facilitating a qualitative analysis of subjects' miscomprehensions and difficulties as may be revealed in their written recall protocols.

Hamsik (1984) found that students trained in ESL classes were reading at close to elementary levels. Furthermore, she found that even those students whose TOEFL (Test of English as a Foreign Language) scores exceed 550 were reading at Flesch level of "Fairly Easy", and are not reading at a level even close to the native English readers' average or standard difficulty level. According to Hamsik (1984), by other read- ability formulae, these subjects are reading similar to the level of sixth or seventh graders (native English readers) in American schools.

WRITTEN RECALL

The emerging consensus among researchers in L1 and L2 reading is that the written recall is a valid and integrative method of assessing retention after readers have read a text (Bernhardt, 1991; Hammadou, 1988; Lee, 1986; Meyer, 1985; Smith &Jackson, 1985;Wells, 1986). It is also a reading comprehension assessment technique that reflects the current conception of the constructive process of reading (Bernhardt, 1986; Kamil, 1986; Hammadou, 1988). A plethora of studies in L1 and L2 reading research have utilized the written recall as a dependent measure of comprehension. The free written recall was found to provide more insightful information than structured questions (e.g., Johnston, 1983). There are many advantages of the recall protocol, one being its ability to provide both quantitative and qualitative information of readers' construction of meaning.

Information provided from recall protocols written in the native language, or language that readers are familiar with has been found to reveal more and better information than protocols written in the target language (TL) or the language the students are learning (Bernhardt, 1986; Lee, 1986). When writing in the second language or in the TL, students tend to focus on grammar, spelling of words, and choice of words and not fully on comprehension (Bernhardt, 1991). The language of recall was the subjects' academic language *(Bahasa Malaysia),* which is the national language of Malaysia. For a majority of the students in the study, who are from the Malay race, *Bahasa Malaysia* is similar to their first language. However, *Bahasa Malaysia* is the standard, formal language of all Malaysians. All the subjects in the study, regardless of ethnic background, have been exposed and schooled in *Bahasa Malaysia* from fifteen to twenty years. The medium of instruction in all schools and institutions of higher learning is in *Bahasa Malaysia.*

THE WRITTEN RECALL PROCEDURE

In a typical free written recall task, readers are given a passage to read. They are instructed to read for understanding. After reading the passage, and upon surrendering the passage to the teacher or instructor, the readers are asked to recall everything that they can remember and have understood of the passage read, in their native language or the language they are proficient in. Readers are given pieces of lined paper to write down their recalls. Readers are reminded to include everything, main ideas and details, and not only to summarize the text read. Readers are also instructed to write in full sentences. In some procedures, to counter short-term memory effects, an unrelated task is given to readers before the actual recall of the passage read.

In this study, the subjects were informed beforehand that they were going to perform on an immediate written recall task. They were informed that they were required to read and understand the passage, and then recall everything that they could remember from the passage. There were no intervening tasks between the reading of the passage and the recall task. The researcher is of the opinion that memory and comprehension factors cannot be separated, and thus joins the ranks of other researchers who view memory and comprehension as closely intertwined (e.g. Royer & Cunningham, 1981).

SCORING WRITTEN RECALL PROTOCOLS

Meyer's (1975) scoring system has been widely used in L1 reading research; however, another scoring system that is found to be as valid is one following that of Johnson's system (1970). Bernhardt (1991) cross- validated the Meyer's (1975) system with that of Johnson's using data from the Allen et al. (1988) study. She found that the latter system is the better system because it does not only provide similar information as that of Meyer's system, but it also utilizes less time and effort, and it is straightforward when compared with Meyer's scoring system. The following procedure was used to develop a scoring template for the study's written recall protocols:

1. The passage was first parsed into "pausal acceptability units" by seven native English speakers-graduate students (doctoral) who were teaching English (ESL) at the Center for Intensive English Studies at The Florida State University. The graduate students were asked to read the passage orally to themselves (as in normal-paced reading), and to put a slash in all those places where they paused. Next, the researcher calculated a reliability estimate of the inter-rater judgements of what constituted a pausal unit or proposition. Inter-rater reliability was found to be at r = .87, but further discussions resulted in a common consensus. Eventually, an overlap of almost one hundred percent was achieved. In one case, a rater provided a slightly longer number of idea units, however, the "more narrower idea units" was taken (Bernhardt, 1996,209).

2. Two additional independent raters (graduate student teachers of ESL at The Florida State University) were asked to read the passage without the slashes. They then discussed and decided as to the passage's main ideas and supporting details. In addition, the two raters discussed and decided the importance of each idea unit as it relates to the whole passage. This was to ensure that both raters fully understood the content of the passage, and also to facilitate agreement among the raters. (E. B. Bernhardt, personal communication, September, 1991). Next, the two raters were each given the passage with slashes in them. They were asked to read the passage again, and then to weigh each proposition following Johnson's (1970) method. That is, the raters were asked to divide the passage into three or four levels: the lowest is the least important 25 percent of the idea units in the text, the next level is the next least important 25 percent, and so on (Bernhardt, 1991).

   Then, raters were asked to assign the value of 1 to the lowest 25 percent, the next a value of 2, the next 3, and finally, the most important information a value of 4. It was found that the passage chosen for this study contained idea units that were amenable to a division of three levels of importance. Level one was for ideas that were of least importance or that were labelled "details". Level two was for less important ideas or ideas that were labelled "supporting ideas". And finally, level three referred to idea units that were considered most important or ideas that were labelled "main ideas".

3. Each idea unit parsed by the pausal acceptability method was then written onto a piece of lined paper, hierarchically, in the order that each appeared in the passage. All the idea units were placed onto the left side of the paper. On the other side of the paper, the value of each unit as to its relative importance to the whole passage, was written corresponding to each idea unit on the left side of the paper.

Example: Idea Unit   Level
    1   Many American holidays are European in origin   1
    2   because many of the people who settled in North America came from Europe 1

These idea units and their weighted values served as the scoring templates for the subjects' written recall protocols. However, the idea units were first translated into *Bahasa Malaysia*, because the students had been asked to write their recalls in the national language. The translation of the idea units was conducted by the researcher and two other qualified translators. The two translators helped to translate the idea units into *Bahasa Malaysia*.

The recall protocols were scored based on the total number of idea units (adding up all idea units present in students' recall using the weighted values). In addition, the percentage of idea units recalled was calculated (number of ideas recalled divided by the total number of idea units in the passage). The number of idea units recalled for each level of importance was also calculated. The purpose was to examine the kinds of information produced within different types of tasks and within different levels of proficiency of students. All written protocols were scored by this researcher and an independent rater. The independent rater was one of the two translators who was trained by the researcher on the use of the scoring template. Because the protocols and scoring instruments were in *Bahasa Malaysia,* a language different from the language of the passage (English), interpretation of meaning units was not conducted in a strict manner. An interrater reliability coefficient was calculated. The initial reliability was found to be 0.90. The researcher and the independent rater met to discuss the areas of discrepancies. After a thorough discussion of the idea units, a final consensus of one hundred percent agreement was achieved.

QUALITATIVE ANALYSIS OF RECALLS

The framework that was used to guide the qualitative analysis of all 81 subjects' recall protocols was Bernhardt's Constructivist Model of Second Language Reading. The components of the model are text-based and extra-text based (see Chapter 7 for a description of the model). The text-based components are word recognition, phonemic/graphemic decoding, and syntactic feature recognition. The extra-text based components are intratextual perception, prior knowledge, and meta-cognition. Evidence for each of these components was based on an analysis of mismatches between the text content and what was contained in subjects' reconstruction of meaning as seen in their written recalls. Readers' recalls were thus compared to the text's content, and through error analysis, the recalls were categorized according to the components of the model. Therefore, through an analysis of the data, evidence for the six components of the model was examined. For instance, following Lee

(1990), data analysis proceeded first with an analysis of text-based factors followed by an analysis of extratext-based factors:

Text-based factors

1. word recognition

    Does the meaning readers assign to a word affect comprehension?

2. phonemic/graphemic decoding

    Does the sound or visual mismatch of words cause readers to mis- assign the meaning of the word and does this mismatch affect comprehension?

3. Syntactic feature recognition

    Is comprehension affected by the relationship between words?

Extratext-based factors

1. Intratextual perception

    Is comprehension affected by the reconciliation of passage parts?

2. Prior knowledge

    Is comprehension affected by readers' knowledge of the world?

3. Metacognition

    Does the reader think about what he is understanding during reconstruction of meaning?

MULTIPLE-CHOICE QUESTIONS

The multiple-choice questions/items were constructed based on each idea unit outlined in the written recall scoring template. That is, because there were 51 idea units in the template, the resulting number of MC questions constructed was 51. This was to ensure equality of the two tests; what students recall in the IWR task would also be probed in the MC task. The multiple-choice questions contained four plausible alternatives. Each distractor was a plausible answer, and was based on information found in the passage. However, only one alternative was the correct and best answer to the question. Items on the multiple-choice test were framed in *Bahasa Malaysia*. The items were reviewed by the two translators who had earlier assisted in the translation of the parsed idea units for the scoring template. Any weak items, in terms of inaccurate wordings and so forth were corrected in the discussions between the two translators and the researcher. The amount of points awarded to the answers in the MC test likewise reflected the weights assigned to the idea units in the IWR scoring template.

Example:

IWR Task	Idea unit	Level
	/many American holidays are European in origin/MC Task	1

What is the origin of most American holidays?

    a.   Indian
    b.   European
    c.   English
    d.   North American

If a student had chosen the correct answer (b), h/she was awarded 1 point (in terms of the importance of the answer relative to the whole passage). Thus, two students may obtain the same score, but each person's score would differ qualitatively. For instance, one student may have obtained mainly details and very little salient information, whereas another may have obtained more of the major ideas, but fewer of the details. However, total scores on the MC test was equivalent to that in the IWR test, since the information tapped from the passage was the same and was given a parallel value in both tests.

Students were instructed to "circle" the number or letter of the correct answer in the directions of the MC task. In this way, students' responses to the questions could be easily analyzed in terms of levels of importance of idea units because the question stems and alternatives were grouped together rather than separated as in a "bubble sheet" response format.

PILOT TESTING OF MC QUESTIONS

The multiple-choice questions were tested on a sample of students from the morning sections of the three courses. These subjects were either from the Islamic or Economics faculty. Four randomly selected intact classes of a total number of 54 students sat for the MC test during the first week of classes in the beginning of the semester (July, 1992). A week later, the same test was given to the same students. Students were not informed earlier that they would be sitting for the same test. Procters in each class were the instructors of the three levels of reading courses of the morning session of classes. The subjects were given 20 minutes to read the passage after which the passage was then surrendered to the class instructor. The subjects were then provided with the answer booklet that contained the MC questions and the four-alternative answers. The time limit for performance on the MC questions was 30 minutes.

A test-retest reliability coefficient was calculated and was found to be at $r = .80$. According to Diederich (1973) and Oosterhof (1990), teacher-made tests conducted within one class period should have a reliability of between .60 and .81. Because the MC pilot test required a full class period (approximately an hour) to complete, the reliability coefficient of .81 was considered by this researcher to be acceptable. Based upon the pilot test result, the researcher decided to use the MC test in the main study. In addition, an item analysis of the test items was conducted. The necessary modification of question stems and distractors was conducted by the researcher and was reviewed by the two hired translators/instructors at the Language Center. The researcher had computed Cronbach Alpha reliability (internal consistency test) on the MC scores of subjects of the main study. The reliability of the MC test was found to be at $r = .825$.

PRIOR KNOWLEDGE MEASURE

To account for subjects' prior knowledge of the passage's topic, subjects in the main study were required to perform on a "topic familiarity" task before reading the passage. Students were given three topics on common American holidays. One of the three was the topic of the test passage - Thanksgiving holiday. To provide students with confidence and motivation to perform the task, two of the topics were on holidays that most students are familiar with, that is, Christmas and Valentine's Day. Students were asked to free-associate; to "write down everything you know or anything that comes to mind about each of these topics". Instructions were in *Bahasa Malaysia* and students were also asked to write in *Bahasa Malaysia*.

The free-association measure has been used with a number of studies to assess the "breadth and depth" (Valencia, Stallman, Commeyras, Pearson, & Hartman, 1991, 210) of topical knowledge (Bernhardt, 1988; Langer, 1980; among others). It has been found that this type of topical knowledge assessment is "strongly related to subsequent recall of passages." (Valencia et al., 1991,210). The judgement of student responses in this study followed that of Bernhardt (1988) and Langer (1980). That is, three levels of prior knowledge were given to the associations that students provide. They are:

1. High prior knowledge was assigned 3 points. This means that the reader is able to produce "superordinate concepts, definitions, analogies, and linking" (Langer, 1980,29).
2. Some prior knowledge was assigned 2 points. This shows that the reader is able to provide "examples, attributes and defining characteristics" (Langer, 1980,29).
3. Low prior knowledge was assigned 1 point. This means that the reader "makes associations with morphemes, sound-alikes, and first-hand experiences" (Langer, 1980, 29).

The students' responses on the free association task were thus scored on this three-point scale. The scores were used to facilitate interpretation of the quantitative and the qualitative analyses of students' written recall protocols and multiple-choice test. The researcher and two bilingual (English/Bahasa Malaysia) instructors at the Language Center scored students' responses on the free-association task.

BIOGRAPHICAL INFORMATION

Each subject was asked to fill out a short biographical information form which comprised such information as age, sex, mother-tongue, Bahasa Malaysia grade (SPM/STPM), and so forth.

PROCEDURES

There were two main packets of materials for the test the IWR packet and the MC packet. The IWR packet contained the expository passage, four pieces of lined paper, a biographical information form, and a topic familiarity form. The biographical information form and the topic familiarity form were attached together, whereas the passage and the lined paper had each appeared separately. The MC packet comprised the expository passage, the multiple-choice questions booklet, the biographical information form and the topic familiarity form. Likewise, the passage and the MC questions booklet were in separate packets. The biographical information form and the topic familiarity form in the MC task packet were attached together.

Once the test packets had been put together, the administration of the experimental test proceeded as follows:

1. The subjects were first informed of the purpose of the study. They were reminded of their rights to anonymity; that their performance on the tests, in terms of scores, would not be released to anyone except to the researcher. Their names would not be used during scoring, only their metric number, or through the use of a coding system developed by the researcher. Each subject was given the packet containing the biographical information form and their topic familiary form by procters recruited for the test (Seven procters were hired by the researcher. Procters included instructors at the Language Center and graduate students in the English program of the university). All written and oral instructions were in *Bahasa Malaysia*. Oral directions during the test were provided through the use of a microphone and speakers that were installed by the university's "technical/materials" services department. Students were given 20 minutes to fill in the two forms.

2. Once the two forms were completed, they were collected by the seven proctors. The subjects were then given the test passage to read. Oral and written instructions (in the passage) directed the students to read and understand the passage. They were reminded that 20 minutes was the time allowed for them to read the passage, after which the proctors would collect the passages. They were also told that some students would perform on a MC task, whereas others would be asked to recall everything in writing in *Bahasa Malaysia*.

3. After surrendering the passage, each student was provided with either the MC booklet or the four pieces of lined paper, depending upon the type of task to which they had been earlier randomly assigned.

The time allowed for the two tasks (MC or IWR) was 30 minutes each. Proctors had collected all papers at the end of the allocated time.

OPERATIONALIZATION OF VARIABLES

INDEPENDENT VARIABLES

There were two independent variables in the study: (a) type of testing method/task, and (b) level of English proficiency. Type of testing method/task was represented by the Immediate Written Recall task (IWR) and the Multiple-Choice task (MC).

"Level of English language proficiency" corresponded to the three levels of reading courses that students were placed into based upon their performance in the English department's ELPT (English Language Proficiency Test) examination. Each level thus reflected a different proficiency level. These two independent variables were measured on a nominal scale.

DEPENDENT VARIABLES

The dependent variables were the two scores on the IWR and MC tasks. Both scores were measured on the same scale. Because the total scores on both tasks were used, the scores were on an interval scale.

ANALYSES

The results of the study were analyzed accordingly, following a procedure appropriate for a 3 x 2 Factorial ANOVA (analysis of variance). The two factors were type of testing method or task and level of English language proficiency. The first factor-type of testing method or task-had two levels: (a) Immediate Written Recall task (IWR), and (b) multiple- choice task (MC). The second factor-level of English language proficiency-had three levels: (a) Level I (corresponding to the reading course VE1003, (b) Level II (corresponding to the reading course VE1043), and (c) Level III (corresponding to the reading course VE1053). Data in the form of scores on the two tests (IWR and MC) were analyzed to address the first three research questions. The F- statistic was computed to investigate whether there were any significant main effects of type of testing method, level of proficiency, and any interactions between these two factors. As part of interpretation, the strength of relationships was also computed by using the omega 2 procedure for any significant main effects and interactions. The omega-square was used because this study had a balanced design (Brown, 1990; Hatch & Lazarathon, 1991).

Research question #1

The first research question addressed the effect of type of testing method or task on students' comprehension scores as measured by the IWR and the MC tasks. An ANOVA with two levels was used to analyze the scores on the two tasks. The null hypothesis for the analysis of the first research question was as follows:

1. There is no difference in reading comprehension mean scores according to testing method.

$$Ho: ulWR = uMC$$

ulWR: the group mean of the IWR group on the IWR test
uMC the group mean of the MC group on the MC test

The alternative hypothesis states that there will be a difference in reading comprehension mean scores according to testing method.

$$Ha: ulWR = Umc$$

Research question #2

The second research question addressed the effect of level of English proficiency on students' comprehension scores on the two tests. The ANOVA with three levels was used to analyze the data. The null hypothesis for the second research question was stated as follows:

2. There is no difference in reading comprehension mean scores according to the three levels of proficiency.

$$Ho: uI = uII = uIII$$

uI = the group mean of the Level I proficiency group on both the IWR and MC tests
uII = the group mean of the Level II proficiency group on both the IWR and MC tests
uIII = the group mean of the level III proficiency group on both the IWR and MC tests

The alternative hypothesis states that there is a difference in reading comprehension mean scores according to the three levels of proficiency.

Research question #3

The third research question addressed the interaction effect of both type of testing methods and level of proficiency on students' reading comprehension scores. The null hypothesis for this research question was as follows:

3. There is no interaction effect between type of testing method and level of proficiency on reading comprehension scores. The alternative hypothesis states that there is an interaction effect between type of testing method and levels of proficiency on reading comprehension scores.

QUANTITATIVE ANALYSIS

DEMOGRAPHICS: SUBJECTS' CHARACTERISTICS

Table 1 displays the descriptive statistics of the participants. The majority of the subjects are female and the average age is 22. In terms of ethnic composition of the sample, the subjects were predominantly Malay. The sample for the study involved students from both the Economics and Islamic departments.

Table 1 Demographics: Mean and Standard Deviation

Variable	Mean	Std Dev	N	Code	n
Ethnic Group	1.18	.50	162	1 = Malay	140
				2 = Chinese	16
				3 = Indian	5
				4 = Aborigine	1
Sex	1.65	.48	162	1 = Male	56
				2 = Female	106
Age	21.86	3,71	162		
Faculty	1.57	.50	162	1 = Islam	69
				2 = Econs	93

The Islamic faculty comprised mainly Malay students and the Economics faculty included some Malay students. Thus, this accounts for the larger number of students from the Malay race. This fact, however, does not introduce bias into the study because the language of the two tests, Bahasa Malaysia, is similar to the language of the Malay people. The 16 Chinese, 5 Indian, and 1 *OrangAsli* (native) subjects, like the Malay subjects, had had about 20 years of education with *Bahasa Malaysia* as the medium of instruction.

BACKGROUND INFORMATION OF SUBJECTS: METHOD, BAHASA GRADE, LEVEL, AND ELPT SCORE

Table 2 displays the means and standard deviations of subjects' Bahasa and English Language Placement Test (ELPT) scores. A total number of 162 subjects participated in the study. From the pool of students in the afternoon session of the three levels of reading courses, 54 subjects were randomly selected from each level. And out of these 54 subjects, 27 were randomly assigned to method 1 (multiple-choice task), and the other 27 were assigned to method 2 (immediate written recall). There was a total number of 81 subjects per method across proficiency levels.

Table 2 Descriptive Statistics: Method, Grade, Level, and ELPT

Variable	Mean	Std Dev	Min	Max	N	Code
Method (METH)	1.50	.50	1.00	2.00	162	1 = IWR 2 = MC
Bahasa Malaysia Grade (BMG)	2.22	.76	1.00	4.00	162	1 = Distinc 2 = High 3 = Credit 4 = Pass
Reading Prof Level (RPL)	2.00	.82	1.00	3.00		1 = Level I 2 = Level II 3 = Level III
English Language Placement Test (ELPD	34.57	7.15	20.00	56.00	162	

DESCRIPTIVE STATISTICS: READING COMPREHENSION AND TOPIC FAMILIARITY SCORES

Table 3 provides a list of the means and standard deviations of subjects' scores on the three tasks in the experiment: the topic familiarity task, the multiple-choice task, and the immediate written recall task. The variable "Score" in the table represents the combination of scores on the MC and the IWR tasks. To reiterate, the two tasks were scored on the same scale and were based upon a single key or scoring template of propositional units or idea units. As can be observed from the table, the mean score obtained by the subjects was 65.14. However, within tasks, by mere observation of the mean score, it is clear that the subjects in the MC method or task had performed better than the subjects in the IWR method. The mean score of the MC method was 86.54 compared to the 43.74 of the IWR method. This score reflected performance across the three levels of reading proficiency.

This score reflected performance across the three levels of reading proficiency. The mean of the topic familiarity task or TF score of the 162 subjects was 1.06. A frequency count was run on the TF scores of all subjects and it was found that 155 subjects obtained a score of one, five subjects obtained a score of two, and two subjects obtained a score of three. This can only mean that a large number of the participants of this study had low or very little background or prior knowledge of the topic of the test passage. Although this was the case, subjects in the MC task seemed to have performed well overall. This low prior knowledge tended to affect the performance of the students in the IWR task. This will be discussed further under the "Qualitative" section of this chapter.

Table 3 Descriptive Statistics: Reading Comprehension and Topic Familiarity Scores

Variable	Mean	Std Dev	Min	Max	N	Code
Score	65.14	25.81	2.00	102.00	162	Score = MCS + IWRS
MCS	86.54	10.97	37.00	102.00	81	MCS = Multiple-Choice Score
IWRS	43.74	17.09	2.00	84.00	81	IWRS = Immed. Written Recall Score
TF	1.06	.28	1.00	3.00	162	TF = Topic Familiarity Score
NMI	8.14	3.34	.00	12.00	162	NMI = Number of Main Units
NSI	18.40	6.44	1.00	28.00	162	.NSI = Number of Supp Ideas
NDT	6.68	2.60	.00	10.00	162	NDT= Number of Details
TNIU	33.21	11.51	2.00	50.00	162	TNIU = Total Number of Idea Units

The mean of the Number of Main Idea units or NMI for all subjects across levels and type of task was 8.14. The total main idea units of the reading passage was 12. Thus, the percentage of NMI units that most subjects obtained was 68 per cent. There was a total of 29 supporting idea units in the reading passage. The mean number of supporting idea units or NSI that subjects obtained was 18.40 or 63 per cent of the total NSI. On the average, subjects obtained 6.68 number of details or

NDT out of the total of ten idea units that was considered "details". This is approximately 67 percent of the total details. And finally, the total number of idea units or TNIU that the subjects obtained, on the average, was 33.21 out of the total of 51 idea units. This is about 65 percent of the total idea units of the test text. However, these idea units were each weighted according to its importance to the whole text. For instance, each main idea unit carried a weight of 3 marks; a supporting idea carried a weight of 2 marks; and a detail carried a weight of 1 mark. Therefore, a subject's score on either one of the two tasks reflected a total of weighted scores. Subjects' performance in terms of the three different idea units within specific tasks (MC or IWR) will be discussed under "Other Questions of Interest" in the following pages.

Research question 1

An analysis of variance was run using the analytical program from the *SPSS/PC + STUDENTWARE PLUS* (SPSS, Inc.,1991) on the reading comprehension scores. Table 4 displays the source table for the ANOVA. There was an effect of type of testing method or task on comprehension scores. That is, there was a Significant difference between the means of the scores of the MC and the IWR (F = 360.2383, df= 1,160, P < .00005). The mean score of students in Group 1 or the MC task was 86.5432 (S.D. = 10.9671), whereas that of the students' in Group 2 or the IWR task was 43.7284 (S.D. = 17.0851).

Subjects in the MC group thus outperformed the subjects in the IWR group. This is probably because the multiple-choice task is far easier than the immediate written recall task. The MC task, as developed for this study, is a recognition and recall task. The IWR, a more demanding task, required subjects to produce in writing what they had understood of the text read. This calls for organization of thought and of high comprehension.

Table 4 Results of ANOVA: Score by Method (MC vs IWR)

Source of Variation	DF	Sum of Squares	Mean Squares	F Ratio	F Prob.
Between Groups	1	74240.8889	74240.888	9360.2383'	.00005
Within Groups	160	32974.1235	206.0883		
Total	161	107215.0123			

*p < .05

To remember everything, subjects need to have understood the content and the meaning of the passage. The result of the ANOVA indicated that in terms of comprehension scores, it made a difference as to the type of testing method that subjects were assigned. Across proficiency levels, the subjects who performed on the MC task did much better than those subjects who had performed on the IWR task. Hence, the null hypothesis of no effect on comprehension scores of type of testing method (MC or IWR) was rejected.

Research question 2

To test the hypothesis of no effect of reading proficiency levels on reading comprehension scores, an ANOVA on the scores was run using the *SPSS/PC* + (SPSS, Inc., 1991) program. The dependent variable was the score, whereas the independent variable was the three reading proficiency levels. The source table of the ANOVA (Table 5) indicated that the F-ratio was less than 1.00 and that the Significance level of F was large, thus the null hypothesis of no effect of proficiency level was not rejected. The B-Tukey multiple range test was computed on the scores at alpha .05 level. The results showed that there were no two groups that were significantly different at the alpha .05 alpha level. The means of the scores of the three reading proficiency levels: Level I, Level II, Level III were 65.0741, 65.9815 and 64.3519 respectively. It seemed thus, that reading proficiency level had no effect on subjects' performance on the comprehension tasks. Across levels, the subjects were performing approximately equally. However, across tasks, the subjects who sat for the MC task outperformed those subjects who sat for the IWR task. Table 6 displays the results of the ANOVA on MC scores and

Table 5 Results of ANOVA: Score by Reading Proficiency Level

Source of Variation	DF	Squares of Squares	Squares Mean	F Ratio	F Prob.
Between Groups	2	72.0123	36.0062	.0534	.9480
Within	159	107143.0000	673.8553		
Total	161	107215.0123			

p < .05

Table 7 illustrates the results of the ANOVA on IWR scores. It can be seen that within the two tasks, as measured by their comprehension scores, all the three groups had relatively equivalent performance.

Table 6 Results of ANOVA: Me Score by Reading Proficiency Level

Source of Variation	DF	Sum of Squares	Mean Squares	F Ratio	F Frob.
Between Groups	2	146.6914	73.3457	.6038	.5493
Within	78	9475.4074	121.4796		
Total	80	9622.0988			

p < .05

Table 7 Results of ANOVA: IWR Score by Reading Proficiency Level

Source of Variation	DF	Sum of Squares	Mean Squares	F Ratio	F Frob.
Between Groups	2	544.8889	272.4444	.9314	.3984
Within Groups	78	22816.6667	292.5214		
Total	80	23361.5556			

p < .05

The B-Tukey Multiple Range test conducted on the two ANOVAs further supported this finding. No two groups were significantly different at the alpha .05 level of Significance. The null hypothesis of no effect of reading proficiency level on subjects' comprehension scores was not rejected.

Research question 3

To answer the third research question of whether there is any interaction between type of testing method or task and reading proficiency level, an ANOVA was computed on the comprehension scores of the subjects.

The two independent variables were type of testing method and reading proficiency level. The results of this 3 x 2 Factorial ANOVA is displayed in the above table (Table 8).

Table 8 Results of Factorial ANOVA: Score by Method by RPL

Source of Variation	Sum of Square	DF	Mean Square	F	Signif of F
Main Effects	74312.901	3	24770.967	119.681	.000
METH	74240.889	1	74240.889	358.696	.000'
RPL	72.012	2	36.006	.174	.840
2-way Interactions METHRPL	614.111 614.111	2	307.056 307.056	1.484 1.484	.230 .230
Explained	74927.012	5	14985.402	72.402	.000
Residual	32288.000	156	206.974		
Total	107215.012	161	665.932		

*P < .05

The source table indicated that there was no significant interaction between the two factors, Method and RPL. There was only a single main effect, which was the effect of type of method or task on comprehension scores. Because the design of this study was a balanced design, the omega-squared was computed to determine the proportion of variability in the dependent variable (comprehension scores) that can be accounted for by type of testing method or task. The omega-squared statistic was found to be 0.6892. In other words, approximately 69 per cent of the variability in the comprehension score could be accounted for by type of testing method.

To examine, in graphic form, the means of the two independent variables (Method by RPL) in the 3 x 2 ANOVA, a line graph and a bar chart are presented in Figures 2 and 3 respectively. From the two figures, it is clear that there was an absence of interaction between Method and Reading Proficiency Level. Whether subjects were in Level I, Level II, or Level III, the MC seemed to be the easier task in contrast to the IWR.

SECONDARY FINDINGS: OTHER QUESTIONS OF INTEREST

A number of secondary findings emerged as a result of the analyses of the data of the main study. In particular, it was found that method had an effect on the number and type of idea units that subjects obtained.

However, reading proficiency level had no effect on the number and type of idea units that subjects obtained. Tables 9 and 10 display the: results of ANOVAs that were computed on the total number of idea units or TNIU that subjects obtained in the two tasks. In terms of total number of idea units, subjects who were in the MC testing method scored higher than the subjects who had sat for the IWR task (Table 9). How- ever, in terms of the three levels of proficiency, there did not seem to be a statistically significant difference in the total number of idea units that subjects obtained (Table 10).

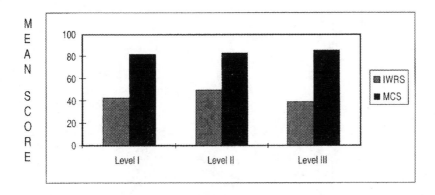

**Figure 2 Comparison of means: Method by proficiency level
(Bar Chart)**

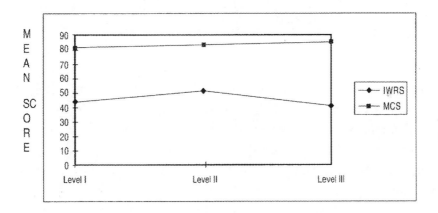

**Figure 3 Comparison of Means : Method by proficiency Level
(Line Chart)**

Table 9 Results of ANOVA: TNIU by Method

Source of Variation	DF	Sum of Squares	Mean Squares	F Ratio	F Prob.
Between Groups	1	12693.5556	12693.5556	235.1391*	*roo*
Within Groups	160	8637.3086	53.9832		
Total	161	21330.8642			

*P < .05

Table 10 Results of ANOVA: TNIU by Reading Proficiency Level

Source of Variation	DF	Sum of Squares	Mean Squares	F Ratio	F Frob.
Between Groups	2	3.7901	1.8951	.0141	.9860
Within Groups	159	21327.0741	134.1325		
Total	161	21330.8642			

p < .05

That is, at all levels of proficiency, all subjects seemed to have obtained a relatively equal amount of number of idea units. A question of interest that was raised as a result of these two analyses was the kinds of effect that type of testing method or task and reading proficiency level could have on the different types of idea units. In this study, there were three levels or types of idea units.

They were main ideas, supporting ideas, and details. They have each been weighted according to their importance to the ideas in the passage as a whole. To answer this question, separate ANOVAs were run on the number of main ideas or NMI, the number of supporting ideas or NSI, and the number of details or NDT. The results of this computations revealed that in terms of NMI, NSI, and NDT, subjects in the multiple- choice testing method outperformed those subjects in the immediate written recall method. There was a statistically significant difference between the MC and and the IWR scores (NMI, NSI, NDT) at alpha less than .05 level. In contrast, within each type of idea units, whether it was NMI, NSI, or NDT, subjects at all the three levels were performing equally. There was no statistically significant difference between the three levels of proficiency in terms of main ideas (NMI), the number of supporting ideas (NSI), or the number of details (NDT). The significance level for these ANOVAs was also at alpha less than .05.

Another question of interest that was raised as a result of the main analyses of the research data pertained to the relationship between the topic familiarity scores or TF and variables in the study such as the comprehension score, the MC and IWR scores, the proficiency level, and faculty. To answer this question, a Pearson Correlation was computed on the topic familiarity scores and the other variables mentioned above. Table 11 is a correlation matrix of the intercorrelations of all the variables. From the correlation matrix, it can be observed that there was no significant linear relationship between topic familiarity and the variables comprehension score, MC and IWR scores, reading proficiency level, and faculty (at alpha less than .0005, two-tailed significance). This can be interpreted to mean that topic familiarity did not affect how subjects performed on the two tasks.

Table 11 Pearson Correlation Coefficient

	TF	*SCORE*	*MCS*	*IWRS*	*RPL*	*FAC*
TF	1.00	.0948	.0245	-.0182	-.0544	.0824
	(162)	(162)	(162)	(162)	(162)	(162)
	P = .	P = .230	P = .757	P = .818	P = .41	P = .297
SCORE	.0948	1.0000	-.8270	.8436	-.0115	.1952
	(162)	(162)	(162)	(162)	(162)	(162)
	P = .230	P = .0	p = .0005	p = .0005	p = .885	P = .013
.MCS	0245	-.8270	1.0000	-.9995	0012	.0158
	(162)	(162)	(162)	(162)	(162)	(162)
	P = .757	P = .0005	p = .	p = .0005	p = .987	P = .842
IWRS	-.0182	.8436	-9995	1.0000	-.0018	-.0045
	(162)	(162)	(162)	(162)	(162)	(162)
	P = .818	P = .000	P = .0005	p= .	p = .982	P = .954
RPL	-.0544	-.0115	.0012	-.0018	1.0000	-.8256
	(162)	(162)	(162)	(162)	(162)	(162)
	P = .491	P = .885	P = .987	P = .982	P = .	P = .0005
FAC	.0824	.1952	.0158	-.0045	-.8256	1.0000
	(162)	(162)	(162)	(162)	(162)	(162)
	P = .297	P = .013	p = .842	P = .954	P = .0005	p = .

(Coefficient / (Cases) / 2-tailed Significance)

" . " indicates a coefficient that cannot be computed.

A quantitative analysis, at this point, did not reveal much about whether knowing something about the topic of a passage facilitates or impedes performance on a comprehension task. This supported the need to further examine in depth the comprehension process of the subjects as they interacted with text. The qualitative analysis of subjects' written recall protocols will be discussed and described later. However, a cursory examination of the means of the scores by topic familiarity indicated that there was a difference, albeit a small one.

This difference was however not statistically Significant. Table 12 provides the means of subjects' scores by topic familiarity. The mean of the scores of the two subjects who had high knowledge of the passage's topic was 83.00. The five subjects who had some prior knowledge of the topic had a mean score of 72.8000. The majority of the subjects who had low knowledge of the topic (155 subjects) obtained a mean score of 64.6581. The means of subjects' scores within tasks (MC or IWR) by topic familiarity were also computed. Likewise, it was found that there was no statistically significant difference in terms of comprehension scores within each task by topic familiarity. The subjects' performance seemed to be relatively equivalent regardless of how much they each knew about the topic of the passage. This could be attributed to the type of topic familiarity task that subjects had performed. Subjects were asked to free-associate or write anything that they could think of about the three topics they were given. One of the topics was the actual topic of the test passage, that is, "Thanksgiving Day".

This method of assessing prior knowledge of a topic may not have been sensitive enough to have captured students' background knowledge of the topic. Multiple-choice questions or short-answer questions could have been more successful in revealing what subjects knew about a topic. However, a possible disadvantage of using MC questions to probe prior knowledge is that questions may serve as cues to students as to the nature of the topic.

Table 12 Summary of Means: Score by Topic Familiarity (TF)

Variable	Value	Label	Mean	Std Dev	Cases
TF	1.00	Low Knowledge	64.6581	25.8699	155
TF	2.00	Some Knowledge	72.8000	24.8032	5
TF	3.00	High Knowledge	83.0000	26.8701	2
Total					162

QUALITATIVE ANALYSIS

Research question 4

The intent of this research question was to examine subjects' written recall protocols for evidence of meaning construction and to investigate any problems that subjects may have encountered in the process of making meaning of the passage. In addition, the purpose was to examine whether the model of second language reading posited by Bernhardt (1986) could help explain the comprehension problems that subjects faced in their attempt to reconstruct the meaning of the text read.

To answer the above questions, all 81 subjects' written recall protocols were examined for evidence of the six factors in Bernhardt's (1986) model. All the protocols were analyzed for errors or mismatches between subject's reconstruction and the passage. Errors, mismatches, or any comprehension problems were classified according to the six components of the Bernhardt (1986) model. In the analysis, it was found that indeed there was a dynamic interplay of one factor with the other factors within the six components of the model, as claimed by both Bernhardt (1991) and Lee (1990).

The following is an explication of a sampling of the protocols according to each of the six components of the Second Language Reading Model:

TEXT-BASED FACTORS

Word recognition. "Does the semantic value a reader assigns to a word affect comprehension?" (Lee, 1990, 134)

A majority of the protocols contained word recognition problems. Subject A interprets the word "origin" to mean "follow". The passage states that: "Many American holidays are European in origin because many of the people ... came from Europe." SubjectA renders it as: Many holidays in America follow that of the holidays in Europe [Translated from Bahasa Malaysia]. The subject also translated "North America" as "selatan Amerika [southernAmerica]. The correct Bahasa Malaysia word for North America is "Amerika Utara [A direct translation would be "America North"]. Subject A seems to be confused with the words "north" and "south".

Subject D also has a translation problem with the word "North America". He/She directly translates "North America" to render "Utara Amerika which means "Northern America". The Bahasa word for it is "Amerika Utara, This is a translation problem. The adjective "north" is used instead of the proper noun. However, the student should recognize from his/her prior knowledge of Bahasa that in Bahasa, North America is written as "Amerika Utara", This, however, seems to be the only word recognition problem that subject D has.

Phonemic/graphemic decoding. "Are there words whose semantic value is misassigned due to a sound or visual mismatch that affects comprehension?" (Lee, 1990, 134)

Subject A reproduces "Thursday" as "Tuesday" because of the phonemic and graphemic similarity of the two words. Subject B has a word recognition problem when h/she uses the word "spring" to refer to "streams". This could be because of the graphemic Similarity of the words. The student must have remembered that "spring" was mentioned, and not knowing the word "streams", s/he linked them together to render "and catch fish at the spring (at the river)". Furthermore, the words "spring", "catch fish", and "streams" had appeared within the same sentence in the passage. This could have caused the subject to link the words together.

Subject C recognizes "chief" to mean "murah" [cheap]. S/he writes: "Squanto came/arrived with 90 with a price that is cheap." The phonemic/graphemic similarity between "chief" and subject's word choice "cheap" led the subject to wrongly interpret the sentence. Furthermore, perhaps because "chief" is pronounced /ci.p/ in Bahasa Malaysia (absence of the phoneme /f/ in Bahasa, except for loanwords) caused the subject to associate "chief" with "cheap".

Syntactic feature recognition. "Does the relationship between words affect comprehension?" (Lee, 1990, 135)

Subject A misrecognizes Thanksgiving date as 14th of November on a Tuesday", whereas in actuality it is stated in the text as "the fourth Thursday of November". The subject does not seem to know the difference between the English ordinal number (serial) "fourth" and fourteenth. Subject B interprets "Squanto as a tribe rather than in reference to an Indian man. The student somehow does not recognize the article "an" in the sentence ... Squanto, an Indian, came to them. "The student also interprets "the fourth Thursday" as "every Thursday the 4th week in the month of November". However, this does not affect the overall meaning of the sentence.

EXTRATEXT-BASED FACTORS

Intratextual perception. "Does internal reconciliation of passage parts affect comprehension?" (Lee, 1990, 136)

Subject A's initial perception of the text influenced his interpretation of subsequent ideas in the passage. For instance, h/she wrote that holidays in America "follow" that of holidays in Europe. Subsequently, h/she thinks that although Thanksgiving Day was celebrated for the first time in America, it was brought to America by the Pilgrims. This infers that Thanksgiving day is not really an American holiday, but one that was brought over to America and celebrated there for the first time in 1621. In the last paragraph of his/her recall, subject A specifically refers to Squanto as the Indian that Americans remember when celebrating Thanksgiving.

Subject A has linked ideas in paragraph three and four to come to this conclusion. The text only mentioned that Thanksgiving is celebrated to remember the early settlers and the Indians who helped them.

Prior knowledge. "Does the reader's knowledge of the world affect comprehension?" (Lee, 1990,137)

Subject A refers to the Pilgrims as "Mubaligh". This is a Bahasa word loaned from the Arabic language. Subject A is a student in the Islamic faculty, and based upon his/her knowledge of Muslims and pilgrimages to Mecca, h/she translates the word "Pilgrims" as "Mubaligh" [preachers or religious people]. The subject also relied upon his/her prior knowledge of English words when h/she thinks of the "New World" as an unknown place to the Pilgrims.

Not knowing what "dessert" means, the subject somehow thinks that pumpkin pie is important enough to have become a symbol of Thanksgiving Day. In this sense, subject's guess is not entirely erroneous because pumpkins are actually common during Thanksgiving, and so are pumpkin pies. However, the text does not mention explicitly that pumpkins are symbolic of Thanksgiving. The subject could have read or seen somewhere about pumpkins and Thanksgiving and thus associated the two ideas. This subject had obtained a score of one in his/her prior knowledge task, which means that his/her knowledge of Thanksgiving is little or very low.

Metacognition. "Does the reader think about what he is reconstructing?" (Lee, 1990, 138)

Subject A indicates that h/she knows that his words "grant feast" is referring to some kind of special occasion. Subject A uses English words instead of Bahasa words because h/she is sure of its meaning although "grant" is an incorrect spelling. In a subsequent sentence, h/she refers to it as a "pesta" [festival].

Subject B writes "daging duck" [duck meat] indicating that h/she is aware of the meaning of the words "duck meat". The subject has inserted correctly an English word within his/her Bahasa sentence, perhaps, because h/she cannot find the exact translation of the English word "duck" but knows what it means.

Subject E obviously knows what the passage is basically about for h/she writes "Thanksgiving Day" as the title of his/her recall. To reiterate, the title of the test passage was deliberately omitted by this researcher as part of the design of the study.

SUMMARY OF FINDINGS

The results of the ANOVA indicated that there was a significant difference between the two methods, IWR and Me. The null hypothesis of no difference between the mean scores of the IWR task and the MC task was thus rejected. The mean scores of the two methods indicated that the multiple-choice task seemed to be the easier task. Subjects from across the three levels of reading proficiency who sat for the MC task had outperformed those subjects who sat for the immediate written recall task. This result supports the findings of other researchers such as Davey (1989), Shohamy (1984), and Wolf (1991) who found in their study that the multiple choice task provided a higher score in contrast to other methods of testing reading comprehension.

Furthermore, because the questions of the MC in this study were framed in the national language, a language of the majority of the subjects, the task became much easier for these subjects. Research by Tan and Ling (1979) indicated that multiple-choice questions posed in the native language or in a language that the subjects are familiar with, facilitated performance on the task. Likewise, the IWR or immediate written recall in this study also required the subjects to produce in their native language or in the language that they are familiar with (i.e. Bahasa Malaysia). Nonetheless, the subjects on the MC task scored higher than those subjects who sat for the IWR As previously mentioned, the IWR is a more demanding task because it demands not just understanding, but also the subjects' skill in organizing their thoughts. In addition, in comparison to the MC task, the IWR requires greater memory capacity and genuine understanding because the subjects have to hold information longer in memory. In the MC task, the question stems and the distractors or options provided cues that facilitated retrieval of information. Furthermore, the MC is a recognition task as opposed to the IWR, which is more of a productive task.

The results of the ANOVA on the scores of subjects in the three levels of reading proficiency suggested that reading proficiency level does not have a significant effect on subjects' performance in the two tasks. A puzzling finding was that even within each proficiency level, no two groups were found to be significantly different in terms of mean scores in the comprehension tasks. Across levels though, in terms of type of task, the MC group had a higher score than the IWR group. However within each task, that is whether MC or IWR, there was no significant difference in performance of subjects between the three levels. In other words, the subjects who sat for the MC had outperformed those subjects who had sat for the IWR regardless of reading proficiency levels. But within the MC or IWR task, all subjects performed relatively equivalently to each other. Therefore, the null hypothesis of no difference between the mean scores of the three reading proficiency levels was not rejected.

The third research question asked whether there was any significant joint effect or interaction between the two factors, type of testing method or task and reading proficiency level, on the subjects' reading comprehension scores. Based on the ANOVA results, it 'was found that there was no statistically significant interaction between type of testing method and reading proficiency level. In other words, there was no specific task that seemed to have affected performance of subjects at any particular reading proficiency level. Of the two factors, only the effect of task was clearly seen across levels and within each task per proficiency level. That is, regardless of whether subjects are in levels one, two, or three, performance on the MC was better than the performance on the IWR. And within each level, for instance, within Level I, the subjects had performed, on the average, better on the MC task than on the IWR task. And within each task, either MC or IWR, the subjects had performed essentially equivalent across the three levels of proficiency.

A logical expectation of the study would be to expect the more proficient readers to outperform the less proficient subjects on the two tasks. And that between the two tasks, the more proficient readers would perform better on the MC or the IWR or, perhaps, even relatively equivalently on the two tasks. This was not what was suggested by the results of this study. Performance on the tasks was related to the type of students who were in the reading courses. It seems that, in general, the Economics faculty subjects had a superior performance to that of the Islamic faculty subjects in terms of type of task. In other words, the subjects from the Islamic faculty had scored, on the average, higher than the subjects from the Islamic faculty on both the MC and the IWR tasks. The discipline of study factor was not part of this study's variable, and as pointed out earlier, a limitation of this study was that random selection of subjects had involved only subjects from the afternoon session of the three levels of reading courses at the university. And these subjects were either from the Islamic faculty or the Economics faculty.

The final research question, in a way, was concerned with testing Bernhardt's (1986) constructivist model of second language reading. The purpose was to examine whether the model could be supported by the data of this study. Specifically, the intent was to find out whether the model of reading, with its six components, could help explain the problems or errors that subjects encounter in their attempt to reconstruct the meaning of the passage read. In so far as evidence is concerned, the data of this study have indicated that the model posited by Bernhardt can indeed be used to describe the kinds of problems that subjects faced in trying to understand what they have read. All the 81 subjects' written recall protocols contained comprehension problems that could be categorized under one or more factors from either the text-based component or the extratext-based component of the model. A review of the data indicated that there was no single factor that could account for a subject's overall comprehension or miscomprehension. Rather, the interaction of more than one factor was involved.

Thus these data support the claim by Bernhardt (1991) and Hammadou (1991) that an array of both text-based and extratext-based factors interact together to influence a reader's comprehension as ascertained by a written recall protocol procedure. As discussed earlier, each factor could become the impetus for other comprehension problems, or could in itself become part of the problem. For example, a word recognition problem can cause a subject to misinterpret the syntax of a sentence, which could in turn affect how the subject perceives the interpretation of that sentence to the whole passage.

Bernhardt's model, when used as a framework in the attempt to dis- cover what and how subjects have understood the meaning of a text, provides a useful and consistent means of looking at readers' understanding. However, a difficulty that arose during the analysis of the data was when an error or mismatch was found to belong to more than one category. For example, in subject F's recall, h/she has used the word "summer" instead of "spring". This can be a word recognition problem, a phonemic/graphemic decoding problem, or a prior knowledge problem. Either the subject did not know at all the word "spring, or h/she was confused with the words "spring" and "summer" because of the similarity in the first letter 'Is" in the words, or perhaps the subject's lack of prior knowledge of the different seasons had misled him/her to think that "spring" is referring to "musim panas" [summer]. In this case, the researcher had reviewed the recall protocol as a whole to detect any inconsistencies that were possibly related to the subject's choice of the words "musim panas" [summer].

In looking at the recall, it was observed that the subject indicated awareness of the seasons, at least in terms of winter, which s/he had mentioned in a preceding paragraph. However, perhaps because subject F is only familiar with "hot" and "cool" weather in her/his country, s/he thus subsequently concluded that after the cold winter, the next season must be summer. Furthermore, because the passage mentioned that Squanto taught the Pilgrims how to plant corn (and the subject possibly rationalized that plants grow in warm weather rather than in cold), subject F linked the ideas together resulting in an erroneous interpretation. Perhaps this is one example that could aptly describe a characteristic of the second language reading model as being "three dimensional and interactive" (Bernhardt, 1985, 26). In this sense, thus, according to Bernhardt (1985), it is difficult to determine "... at which point in a reconstruction one component influences another one ..." (p. 26). In subject F's recall, for example, prior knowledge or lack of prior knowledge could have influenced his/her word recognition ability, or word recognition or misrecognition itself could have instantiated his/her prior knowledge.

This is a minor problem that can be resolved through a thorough examination of a reader's recall protocol. The advantages of using the Bernhardt model to explain readers' miscomprehensions far outweigh this minor disadvantage. It must be realized that no one factor is mutually exclusive in this interactive reading model; therefore, in the attempt to classify readers' errors or mismatches, a researcher or teacher needs to examine carefully the recall in its entirety to decide to which component the error or problem belongs.

CHAPTER 8

ASSESSING UNDERSTANDING: THE IMMEDIATE WRITTEN RECALL

For ESL students throughout the world, the ability to read in English is paramount to success both in the academic and the outside world. Success often requires the students to display their ability to read and understand a text in some standardized examinations. In some institutions of learning, tests of ESL reading, in general, play a major role in determining whether a student is successful or otherwise. Important placement and evaluation decisions are based upon a student's success or failure on reading tests. Therefore, tests that attempt to assess students' ESL reading comprehension need to be not only valid and reliable, but they need to be fair to the students. These tests should reflect what students do in their daily reading of texts within their curriculum, because in students' everyday academic lives, what they do when they read texts is essentially read and understand the text and then use this information for some purposes. To understand any text read, the students must interact with the text, that is, to reconstruct meaning based upon information in the text and information that the students already possess.

The immediate written recall is a type of testing method that reflects what occurs when students read. It reveals the result of the interaction between the reader and the text. The study provides evidence that supports the IWR task as an alternative tool in the assessment of ESL reading comprehension. The IWR task provides information about what and how the students have understood of the text read. It therefore provides both quantitative and qualitative information about the product of the interaction between reader and text. Preparation of the instrument to test comprehension via the IWR is not a difficult and time-consuming task. A passage is chosen, and it is parsed according to "pausal acceptability units" whereby proficient native speakers of English read the text and put a slash at boundaries where they normally pause in oral reading. An inter-rater reliability is obtained to ensure that the parsing of the text is carried out in a consistent manner. Next, other independent raters prioritize each idea unit to the whole text.

In other words, each idea unit parsed is weighted according to its importance to the ideas in the whole passage. A scoring template is thus prepared based upon these weighted idea units. Students' written recall protocols are then scored using this scoring template. The language of recall can either be in the second language or in the native language or in the language that the reader is most familiar with. However, various studies have indicated that use of the native language or familiar language facilitates recall (Lee, 1986; Lutjeharms, 1982; Tan & Ling, 1979; among others). This is because the reader is unable to recall well in a language that h/she is still learning. It was indicated in this study (Maarof, 1993) that language of recall does affect the quality of recall. For example, subject 157 had recalled first in the second language, English, and subsequently decided to produce his/her recall in his/her native language. Analysis of the subjects recall revealed that the recall protocol in the native language was more consistent and logical and far better than the English recall.

In scoring the IWR, testers need to employ a liberal approach because of the nature of recall whereby it is not possible for everything to be recalled verbatim. For instance, recall that displays sufficient gist to the meaning of the idea unit or proposition is considered acceptable. To ensure consistency of scoring, scorers must have been informed or trained in the scoring technique. Any discrepancies can be resolved through a discussion. Recall protocols can also be scored according to other systems. For instance, testers can use a holistic method of scoring whereby a set of criteria is established to determine levels of the richness of retellings (see Irwin & Mitchell, 1983); through the use of a rating sheet that contains outlines of the ideas in a passage (generalizations, supporting ideas, details, etc.); by assigning weights to each idea unit (see Smith & Jackson, 1985); or through the use of Meyer's (1985) hierarchical structure system of lexical units (see also Bernhardt, 1991). However, this researcher has found the pausal acceptability scoring system of Johnson (1970) to be the most efficient. Bernhardt (1991) provides a thorough description of the advantages of the pausal acceptability scoring system in her book entitled *Reading Development in a Second Language (1991).*

The advantages of the IWR protocol as a method in assessing reading comprehension are many and have been discussed in chapter three. The IWR protocol is amenable to a quantitative analysis that yields a score that serve as numerical evidence of a reader's performance on a reading comprehension test. In that sense, it provides a numerical value much like the conventional multiplechoice questions test. However, because "... a score is a score is a score." (Bernhardt, 1991,219), the IWR protocol has the advantage over the multiple-choice test in that it is able to provide additional qualitative information about a reader's understanding of the text read.

Of course, this is assuming that the tester is interested in truly finding out about whether the reader has really understood what h/she has read. The results of this study indicate that the multiple-choice test and the IWR test are tapping different kinds of information. The demands required of each are different, and as could be seen from the results of the quantitative and qualitative analyses, the information gained from the two tests was also different. Through the quantitative analysis, it was observed that both tests yielded scores in the form of total number of idea units and total weighted idea units that each subject could recall. However, the qualitative analysis of the IWR revealed that the subjects' understandings or attempts to understand were influenced by features of texts and features within the readers themselves. Therefore, because these two tests tap essentially different kinds of information, it can be suggested that some form of multiple-measures of comprehension should be used to assess reading comprehension of ESL students. This is to ensure that a global and comprehensive assessment of comprehension is achieved. To further refine the measurement of comprehension, an assessment of comprehension should also include an oral interview that examines the answers that students provide in the test. This is not feasible though for large-scale testing, but in cases where in depth information is needed such as in reading research and in diagnostic evaluation, this technique would be most beneficial.

The IWR can also be utilized in the construction of MC questions, as has been used in this study (Maarof, 1993). Based upon the idea units parsed by the pausal acceptability technique, a researcher or test developer could develop a variety of multiple-choice questions. Each question could be weighted according to the relative importance of the answer (idea unit) to the content of the text as a whole. In addition, a pilot test could be carried out with a sample of students using the IWR. Based upon the students' recall protocols, the researcher or tester could obtain an overall picture of the kinds of ideas that the students produce. The difficulty level of the text could also be determined by examining the students' protocols. In this way, not only will it be more efficient to construct the MC questions, but also the readability of the text could be accurately estimated according to the proficiency level of the students.

It can be argued that preparation of any assessment instruments is a time-consuming process. Even in the preparation of MC questions, the test developers and teachers have to confer among a committee of several other test developers and teachers to arrive at acceptable questions and answers. This often requires hours of "vetting sessions" whereby evaluators and teachers each construct questions, answers, and distractors. Discussions upon discussions then ensue to which finally the committee will arrive at a consensus as to which items are acceptable or otherwise. In addition to that, the completed test would have to be tested on a sample of students to determine the test's reliability and validity.

The preparation of the IWR testing technique does not require such a rigorous procedure. Texts are chosen and parsed by native speakers or near-native speakers who are proficient in English. Next, the idea units are assigned weights according to their relative importance to the whole text. Once the scoring template is ready, the passage is given to the students to read. The recall protocols are then compared to the scoring template for absence or presence of idea units of the passage in students' recalls. Besides that, a qualitative analysis of the protocols could assist evaluators and teachers in the development of reading programs or for placement decisions.

Nevertheless, there are those who will argue against using the IWR as a testing technique for fear of not getting a simple, single, objective answer to a test question. However, comprehension is not that simplistic. It is a complex, internal, and elusive process that depends upon an array of interacting factors within the reader and the text, as concurred by various researchers and educators in various fields of learning. Until such time when the comprehension process can be thoroughly described to reflect exactly what occurs when a reader reads and comprehends, researchers and educators must continue in the search for an accurate and valid means of asssessing readers' comprehension.

At present, all reading comprehension measures remain indirect indicators of comprehension. Nonetheless, among many of these measures, the IWR has been found to be a valid and useful means of describing what problems readers encounter in their attempt to understand a text. This study has provided evidence to support the viable use of the IWR as a construct valid testing tool in the assessment of ESL reading comprehension. This researcher, however, joins other researchers and reading educators in the call for the use of multiple-measures in asssessing reading comprehension. In other words, the IWR protocol should be used together with the multiplechoice test, the doze, and other measures of comprehension so that a comprehensive picture of a reader's understanding could be captured.

CHAPTER 9

IMPLICATIONS FOR TEACHING AND RESEARCH

The results of the study conducted by Maarof (1993) attempts to provide some pedagogical implications for the language teacher. The fact that the students have been placed in a class based upon their performance on some placement test does not solve the teacher's problem. The teacher needs to find out about each student's reading capability and the extent of the student's ability to read in the second language. It is in such a situation that the IWR protocol can be used to determine each student's strengths and weaknesses. In cases when the student class population comprises a homogeneous group of students speaking a common native language, the teacher can allow the students to recall in their native language when writing their recalls. The teacher could then use an error classification method to categorize student's errors found in their recalls. For instance, as used in this study, Bernhardt's model of second language reading was used as a framework to help categorize the mismatches or errors that the readers made in their recalls.

Based upon the analysis of recall protocols, the teacher is able to learn about the different problems that a student may encounter in trying to reconstruct his/her understanding of the text. Some of these problems could either be text-based or extratext-based in nature. Once the teacher is aware of the specific problems that students are facing, the teacher can then use this information to modify his/her instruction for these students. In addition, as suggested by Berkemeyer (1989), teaching strategies such as preparing students for different reading purposes would make reading more productive for the students. One such strategy is providing students with the appropriate background knowledge before they read such as in prereading activities. Background knowledge provided would have to be specific to the text that is about to be read. Otherwise, students may not be able to instantiate relevant information to relate to the ideas in the text.

Another instructional strategy would be to instruct the students to use metacognitive or thinking strategies. For example, based upon the analysis of a student's recall, if it was found that the student has intra- textual perception problems, the teacher could assist the students in the technique of rereading and reassessing what has been read. The student could be encouraged to read using the different reading skills such as skimming, scanning, and reading for details. The teacher could include a variety of activities that could reinforce the reading skills that students have been taught, such as matching titles to different reading texts, summarizing ideas, and so forth (See Day, 1993) for a collection of various activities and tasks for use to teach reading.

Beginning instruction this way will lead both the teacher and student towards a more successful endeavor. The teacher will be well-informed of the students' reading problems, and the student will be made aware of the problems he/she is facing in reading. The students could then assist the teacher in facilitating instruction. And the teacher in turn, could facilitate the students in learning to read. Instruction and learning become an interactive and reciprocal process for both students and teacher.

In sum, based upon the results of the study (Maarof, 1993) it was found that the IWR protocol is a valid and useful instrument that reveals the quantity and quality of information that readers produce in their construction of meaning after reading a text. The data from this study also serve as empirical evidence to support the second language reading model proposed by Bernhardt (1986). The model has been found to be a useful framework in the analysis of readers' reconstruction of meaning after reading a text.

In addition, from the perspective of testing ESL reading, both multiple-choice questions and written recalls could be used to complement each other to achieve a comprehensive picture of readers' comprehension. Because the MC is an easier task, it seems more appropriate to recommend its use for large-scale, norm-referenced tests. However, in cases whereby testers or teachers need to discriminate between individuals or among specific skills, a more discriminating and difficult task such as the IWR would be most appropriate. Pedagogically, the IWR, if used as a diagnostic tool for the purposes of either evaluation and instructional purposes, will provide a wealth of information for the tester and the teacher. Results of recall protocols could be analyzed and could then serve as important data to assist evaluators and teachers in making crucial placement or instructional decisions.

CHAPTER 10

PORTFOLIO: ALTERNATIVE ASSESSMENT IN SECOND LANGUAGE READING

The changing face of reading assessment

Reading assessment is undergoing extensive transformations in order to reflect changes that have taken place in the way reading is being defined and in the ways it is being taught. Classroom assessment procedures, those used by classroom teachers on an ongoing basis, are also changing. Less emphasis is being placed in formal test measures and more emphasis is given to teacher observations, samples of students instructional products and student self evaluation. This is because traditional testing cannot accommodate the student who is creative and has an alternative reading of the task. With traditional test, there is a standard 'right answer' and a basis for sorting student into categories or grades. According to Murphy and Smith (1991), the category that the students fall into is decided by how closely their performances match the predetermined 'ideal'. Many students drum up 'right' answers and write essays to a tick of a clock. They are mere recipients of topics and tests. They respond mechanically, taking in facts and echoing them back. These students function as reproducers of knowledge rather than producers.

Assessment must be grounded in current understanding of individual and institutional learning. The assessment activities must enable productive engagement of the disjuncture and foster productive use of the data (Johnston & Costello, 2005). As educators we must remember that the aims of assessment are to identify each student's levels of literacy and develop the student's critical literacy.

The assessment practices need to be representative of the current thinking and practices of our young readers. Readers are no longer passive recipients of knowledge. There is an element of empowerment provided to these readers to allow them to produce reflections or reactions to the reading tasks. Assessment tasks should provide students with the necessary information and skills applicable to the real–world context.

Shaklee (1997) states that portfolio assessment as a practical strategy in organizing developmental record of the student's performance and progress has now emerged as a very important innovation in the scheme of assessment reform. Portfolios provide a better alternative in terms of seeing through the student growth and progress in a particular skill. Portfolio provides information on what the student has learned, how the student has learned and what that has helped this student learn. Portfolio is one vehicle to encourage and promote thinking.

Definition of portfolio

According to Hill (2005), a portfolio is a systematic collection of student work and reflections that help paint a picture of a whole child. These reflections of work should illustrate growth, significant accomplishments and a student's range of abilities. The activities and the portfolio process transforms teaching and learning to be more learner and outcome oriented.

With the emergence of technology in classroom, portfolios have now adopted a new shape. Web-based portfolios are emerging as assessment tools that provide ongoing development and interaction capabilities (Donna, Cole, Kick, & Mathies, 2000). Moersch & Fisher (1996) put forward the notion that emergence of electronic portfolio on the educational landscape is the result of two major innovations–one pedagogical and the other technological. This new breed of assessment strategies extends beyond paper–pencil format. This form of assessment embraces a wide variety of media (pictures, sound, video, and computer based multimedia presentations) to document students' success across the curriculum.

E-portfolios are a valuable learning and assessment tool. Barret (2003) defines an e-portfolio as a digitized collection of artefacts including demonstrations, resources, and accomplishments that represent an individual, group, or institution. This collection can be comprised of text-based, graphic, or multimedia elements archived on a Web site or on other electronic media such as a CD-ROM or DVD. An e-portfolio is more than a simple collection. It can also serve as an administrative tool to manage and organize work created with different applications and to control who can see the work. E-portfolios encourage personal reflection and often involve the exchange of ideas and feedback. Richards (2005) further posits that e-portfolio is a collection of student work assembled to provide a representation of student achievement. Donna et al. (2000) reinforces that multimedia portfolios can add an important complement to the total assessment of the learner. She further adds that traditional techniques can no longer provide a clear evaluation of desired learning outcomes. Portfolio permits instruction and assessment to be woven together in a way that more traditional approaches do not (Paulson & Paulson, 1996). Fogarty, Burke, & Belgrad (1996) further add that portfolio engages students in constructing a story and a long term account of what and how they learn.

Portfolio localized in the Malaysian Classroom

Portfolios are practical assessment tools for Malaysian schools. Mohd Asri (n.d.) in his study, mentioned that majority of the students believed that they were able to see and identify their weakness. These students also were able to instil a sense of ownership. Through the use of portfolios the researcher was able to diagnose students' skill and competencies, preferences and styles. These findings help educators to make the appropriate and necessary adaptation in teaching. Nasirun (n.d.) further adds that portfolio assessment provides students with more freedom to learn. The flexibility allows the teachers more room to plan their lesson which will not be too exam-oriented.

Elango, Jutti and Lee (2005) elaborate on a study conducted on 143 medical students in International Medical University, Malaysia. The study indicates that these medical students perceive writing portfolio as a useful learning tool. However the study also found that the portfolio tasks were stressful because students leave their work to the very end of their rotation.

In Ying's (2002) study conducted on Malaysian teacher trainees undergoing a diploma course, the findings show that there is a potential of coursework through portfolio in portraying and enhancing student learning. She suggests that portfolio can become an avenue for enhancement of reflective thinking among student teachers or trainees. Hiang (1997) also found that the method of portfolio evaluation suitable for the 331 Year Five students from ten primary schools.

Portfolio for an ESL Reading Class

Portfolio can provide opportunities for meaningful engagement in teaching and learning. The teacher in the class can design the portfolio task to suit the needs of the curriculum and her learners. To cater to the different areas of language, portfolio can be used to depict the various developmental stages of the students. This section describes the use of portfolio in an English as a Second Language reading classroom.

The development and the implementation of portfolio need scrutiny and adequate concern because portfolio data presents a broader and genuine picture of student learning (Melograno, 1996). Hence it is crucial that the designing and execution of portfolio tasks should reflect the desired the learning outcome. The following describes the proposed stages in developing portfolio task.

1. IDENTIFYING TEACHING GOALS

The very first and most important part of organizing portfolio assessment is to decide on the teaching goals (Kemp & Toperoff, 1998). These goals will guide the selection and assessment of students' work for the portfolio. By asking questions such as "What do I want the students to learn?" can help direct the teacher to identify appropriate teaching goals which can be assessed through the students' learning outcomes. The teacher can choose several goals to focus on; for example, general goals such as improvement in independent reading and specific goals such as scanning a text or telling a story.

2. SELECTION OF PORTFOLIO CONTENTS

Selection is to abandonment as collection is to abundance. Decisions must be made about the context and contents of the portfolio based on the content and purposes that the portfolio serves (Fogarty et al., 1996). Kemp and Toperoff (1998) suggest two types of items. The core items are items that the students have included in their portfolio. The core items will be required for each student and will provide a common base from which to make decisions on assessment. The optional items are items of the student's choice. These items will reflect the student's uniqueness and creativity. Students can choose to include not only their "best" pieces of work, but also a piece of work which gave trouble or one that was less successful. Explanations on the choice of the selection should be provided.

Klenowski (2002) suggests that the portfolio used to support learning and teaching should include content selected by the student, teacher and in collaboration with the teacher and student. Class discussions can be carried out to generate the list of core items as well as optional items. Through these discussions, the students will be able to apply creative and critical thinking which will enable them to practice thoughtful learning.

Among the items that can be included in the portfolio are as follows:-

- letters, stories, journal articles, poems
- videotapes of role playing activities
- literature response sheets
- graphic organizers (webs, charts, timelines, character sketches)
- reading logs

REFLECTION STAGE

The final stage in portfolio development is reflection. Kemp and Toperoff (1998) propose that reflection can appear in different stages of the learning process. The reflection can be used for summative as well as formative evaluation. For the purpose of reflection, the learners can prepare a brief rationale for choosing item that should be included. This could relate to the students' performance, to their feelings regarding their progress and/or themselves as learners. Students can choose to reflect upon some or all of the following:

- What did I learn from it?
- How did this learning help me improve my learning?
- What did I do well?
- Why (based on the agreed teacher-student assessment criteria) did I choose this item?
- What do I want to improve in the item?

- How do I feel about my performance?
- What were the problem areas?

Portfolio Assessment – Ipsative Assessment

According to Mabry (1999), ipsative assessment involves judging a students performance on the basis of his or her relative strengths and weakness, skills and knowledge, progress over time, opportunity to learn, interests, goals, academic and personal background and any other known factors that may affect performance. Ipsative assessment does not focus on whether a student has learned a given curriculum and it does not facilitate comparisons among students as much as it generates a fuller understanding of each student and an appreciation of his or her unique accomplishments.

This form of assessment is more personalized and this form maximizes the opportunities to recognize and credit what the students know rather that comparing their achievement to others. Portfolio assessment can be based on ipsative assessment as the portfolio content reflects student's growth and progress over time. Furthermore, the students select their own reading materials. This selection indicates the students thought processes and critical thinking especially when the student is required to provide justification on their choice of reading materials.

The development of the student can be monitored and assessed based on the student's selection and reflection on the core items or reading materials. The portfolio assessment system should allow students to showcase their accomplishments and at the same time require them to make informed decisions and judgments about their quality of work. By reflecting on their own learning (self assessment), students begin to identify the strengths and weakness in their work. These weaknesses then become improvement goals. This too can improve the student's attitude toward reading as a lifelong pursuit.

Quality of portfolio is directly attributed to the quality of feedback provided to the students. Teacher observation is probably one of the best ways to identify non-achievement factors such as efforts, behaviour and attendance to detail (Tileston, 2004). Costa and Kallick (1995) state that portfolio can significantly reduce our dependence on narrow and simplistic forms of assessment. However, there is a need to shift from assessment as a reductive process towards assessment that enriches our knowledge of student work and informs students themselves of their own strength and areas needing improvement. Melograno (1996) suggests the use of commentary sheets by the teacher included in each portfolio. The commentary sheets consist of teacher comments, which provide explanation about the context and focus of the work, description of how the work fulfils the expectations and explanations on how the judgements were made. Commentary sheets may include the following:

a. clarification about the content and focal point of the work
b. explanation about the agreed features of performance in work
c. account about how the work fulfils expectations
d. explanation about how judgement were made

Conclusion

There is a need to provide alternative means of assessment especially in the area of reading. Reading is a skill that requires long term portrayal of students' progress and work. The reading performance of a student cannot be captured in a single snap shot. Continual feedback can help provide teachers to make informed diagnostic and curricular decisions to overcome discrepancies in the reading programmes. Hence the reading assessment tasks should be designed to encourage and highlight self awareness as crucial in developing effective thinkers and learners. This can be carried out using the reflections and providing students with opportunities to carry out independent learning. This will indeed show promise in reducing the artificiality associated with schoolwork as students are more engaged in purposeful tasks and meaningful activities.

APPENDIX A

READING PASSAGE

Many American holidays are European in origin because many of the people who settled in North America came from Europe. They brought their holidays with them to the New World. Thanksgiving Day, however, is a truly American holiday. It started in America. The first Thanksgiving Day was in 1621 in what is now Massachusetts. The people who celebrated the first Thanksgiving were the Pilgrims.

The Pilgrims sailed from England to America on a boat named the MayFlower. They left England because they were unable to practice their religion in the way that they desired. Therefore, they wanted to settle in a new land.

The Pilgrims arrived in the New World in the winter of 1620. Soon after they arrived, Squanto, an Indian, came to them. He showed them how to build houses for the winter. The winter was cold and the settlers did not have much food. Nearly half of them died.

In spring, Squanto taught the settlers how to plant corn and how to catch fish in the streams. The settlers soon had plenty of food. They were thankful to God and to the Indian Squanto for his help. To show their gratitude, they invited the chief of the Wapanoag Indians to a grand feast. The chief brought 90 Indians and together with the settlers, they ate corn, duck, and deer meat.

This celebration is now a tradition. Every year, on the fourth Thursday of November, people in the United States celebrate Thanksgiving. On this day, families come together for a traditional dinner of roast turkey, cranberry sauce, and vegetables. Dessert on Thanksgiving Day is usually pumpkin pie, made from an American plant.

Thanksgiving Day is a time for Americans to give thanks, to be with their families and friends, and to remember the early settlers of their country and the Indians who helped them.

Adapted from *Ready to Read* by Ruth Brancard and Jeanne Hind.
Copyright (c) 1989 by Oxford University Press.

APPENDIX B

Weighted Idea Units/Scoring Template (English)

Level	dea Unit
1	/Many American holidays are European in origin/
1	/because many of the people who settled in North America came from Europe/
1	/They brought their holidays with them to the NewWorld/
3	/Thanksgiving day, however, is a truly American holiday/
2	/It started in America/
2	/The first Thanksgiving Day was in 1621/
2	/in what is now Massachusetts/2
2	/The people who celebrated the first Thanksgiving were the Pilgrims/
2	/The Pilgrims sailed from England to America/
1	/on a boat named the MayFlower/
2	/They left England/
3	/because they were unable to practise their religion/
2	/in the way they desired/
2	/Therefore, they wanted to settle in a new land/
2	/The Pilgrims arrived in the New World/
2	/in the winter of 1620/
2	/Soon after they arrived, an Indian came to them/
1	/Squanto/
2	/he showed them how to build houses/
2	/for the winter/
2	/The winter was cold/
2	land the settlers did not have much food/
2	/Nearly half of them died/
2	/Squanto taught the settlers to plant corn/

2	land how to catch fish in the streams/
2	/In spring/
2	/The settlers soon had plenty of food/
3	/They were thankful to God/
2	/land to the Indian Squanto/
2	/for his help/
2	/they invited the chief of the Wapanoag Indians to a grand feast/
2	/to show their gratitude/
1	/The chief brought 90 Indians/
2	/and together with the settlers/
1	/they ate corn/
1	/duck/
1	/deer meat/
3	/This celebration is now a tradition/
3	/Every year/
3	/on the fourth Thursday of November/
3	/people in the United States celebrate Thanksgiving/
3	/On this day, families come together for a traditional dinner/
2	/of roast turkey/
2	/cranberry sauce/
2	/vegetables/
2	/Dessert on Thanksgiving Day is usually pumpkin pie/
1	/made from an American plant/
3	/Thanksgiving Day is a time for Americans to give thanks/
3	/to be with their families and friends/
3	/and to remember the early settlers of their country/
3	/and the Indians who helped them/

Total Number of Idea Units: 51

Most Important/Main Ideas (Level 3): 12 x 3 = 36

Less Important/Supporting Ideas (Level 2): 29 x 2 = 58
Least Important Ideas/Details (Level 1): 10 x 1 = 10
Total Weighted Idea Units: 104

APPENDIX C

A SAMPLE OF UNEDITED IWR PROTOCOLS

(ENGLISH TRANSLATION)

Protocol A

Subject # 027 (Level I)
IWR Score: 52

Most holidays in America follow that of the holidays in Europe. This is because many of the people in Europe immigrated to the south of America. As for the holiday that celebrates thanksgiving it is a holiday that is celebrated for the first time in America that is in Massachusetts in 1621. The people who brought the holiday were the *Mubalicjh* (pilgrims). They immigrated from Europe to America because they could not perform their religious practice in their own way. Thus they then immigrated to search for new land.

They sailed on a ship that was given the name Mayflower and arrived in a new land that was unknown. There they met an Indian named Syanto. Therefore they asked for that man's help to build their houses. Also at that time it was "rnusim sejuk" (winter). Therefore they did not get enough food and half of them died of starvation.

Then in the Spring season they asked once again for Syanto's assistance to help show them or to learn from that man to plant corn and to catch fish. Thus they could then find their own food. As a sign of repaying the Indian man's kindness they invited the Indian tribe to a "grant feast." As many as 90 Indians came to celebrate together the festival. They prepared a serving of deer meat, duck and corn.

A celebration like this has become a tradition for the American society. They every year would celebrate this holiday on the 14th of November Tuesday. On this day they will prepare a meal such as vegetables, roast chicken and dessert that is served is "pumpkin pie" that is ingredients from vegetables.

On this day they will gather together with their families and friends while enjoying the meal. They also celebrate this holiday as a sign of remembering the first irmnigrant who came to America and the Indian man named Syanto.

NMI: 7/12 (59%)
NSI: 19/29 (66%)
NDT: 6/10 (60%)

Protocol B

Subject # 077 (Level II)
IWR Score: 55

Many holidays that are celebrated in United States of America originate from European countries. However Thanksgiving Day truly originates from the country United States of America. Actually this Thanksgiving Day holiday was started by the Pilgrim people who originate from England in the year 1621 which was at that time in Massachusetts. That is in the north of United States of America.

The Pilgrim people arrived in the north of United States of America in the year 1620 on a ship named Mayflower. At the time they arrived it was the cold season. The Indian people that is the Squanto tribe willingly taught the Pilgrim people build cold season houses. Although it was that half of the immigrant Pilgrims died of hunger because there was no food.

However, after that the Squanto tribe taught the Pilgrim people how to plant corn and to catch fish in spring (in the river). In the end the Pilgrim people had much food and could live an easy life. They were very thankful to God and to the Squanto tribe who showed and taught them. To show their appreciation toward the Squanto tribe who were willing to extend to them a helping hand. The Pilgrim people invited the chief of the Indian tribe from Wapanoag to attend a feast that was held. The chief of the Indian tribe led an entourage of 90 people to attend the feast. They ate corn, "duck" and "deer" meat.

"Thanksgiving" Day celebration has become a tradition at present. Every Thursday the 4th week in the month of November is Thanksgiving Day holiday for the people of United States of America. On that day, they will thank each other especially toward family members and their friends. The food item on that day is usually "froast turkey" "cranberry sauce" and vegetables. The celebration symbol is pumpkin pie.

Today the holiday is used to remember the Indian tribels kindness that is Squanto who had willingly extended help to ass'ist them as well as to remember the immigrant's hardships at that time.

NMI: 5/12 (42%)
NSI: 19/29 (66%)
NDT: 7/10 (70%)

APPENDIX D

CLASSIFICATION OF ERRORS/MISMATCHES VIA BERNHARDT'S MODEL

TEXT-BASED FACTORS

Word recognition. Does the semantic value a reader assigns to a word affect comprehension? The following are sample recalls of subjects that provide evidence for this component.

Subj. 001: Student doesn't recognize the word "settlers". Thinks it refers to another group of people besides the Pilgrims. Student isn't familiar with the word "streams". Thinks it means "sea".

Subj. 015: "origin" interpreted to mean "based upon"

Phonemic/Graphemic Decoding. Are there words whose semantic value is misassigned due to a sound or visual mismatch that affects comprehension?

Subj. 007: "Indian" interpreted to mean "Indian from India" C ... seorang yang berbangsa India ...)

Subj. 010: "new land" interpreted as "new island" C ... pulau yang baru ...).

Syntactic Feature Recognition. Does the relationships between words affect comprehension?

Subj. 112: Student consistently writes "indian" without capitalizing the first letter i". Student doesn't recognize that "Indian" is a proper noun.

"spring" is spelled as "springs" with the plural "s" morpheme. Perhaps this is a feature that is due to interference from student's native language. Student seems to have over- generalized the 'Is' plural morpheme. Plurality is marked differently in Bahasa from that of English. e.g. "books" is rendered "buku-buku" [buku = "book"]. Thanksgiving date as "Thursday, 4 November". Student interprets the sentence ... pumpkin pie made from an American plant. "as ... pumkin pie and American vegetables."

EXTRATEXT-BASED FACTORS

Intratextual perception. Does internal reconciliation of passage parts affect comprehension?

Subj. 001: It is clear from student's overall recall that s/he has misinterpreted the message of the text, and has understood the content according to his/her own perception built on misinterpretations. Student's misinterpretations are results of such problems as word recognition, syntactic feature recognition, and prior knowledge. All these factors together influence the way student reconciles ideas between paragraphs. Because of these problems, intratextual perception errors plagues student's recall. The student attempts to follow closely the structure of the text. H/She starts h/her recall by linking ideas in paragraphs 1 and 2. Student writes that Thanksgiving is a holiday celebrated by both the Europeans and the Americans, and that at present it is celebrated by the "North Europeans". Student's initial perception is already a misinterpretation. Also, student thinks that Thanksgiving has given these people a "new life". Student thinks that Thanksgiving is now celebrated in 1621 in the "New Land". "new land" is recalled as a proper noun. From paragraphs 2,3, and 4: Student thinks that the settlers prevents thieves from stealing their food.

Paragraphs 3 and 4 of the text is actually an explication of how the Pilgrims and the Indians met, and how it eventually led to the celebration of the feast that has now become a tradition among Americans. In trying to reconcile the ideas in these two paragraphs, student's prior knowledge of "Indians and Cowboys" could have impacted his/her recall. Student further states that Thanksgiving is celebrated by the American people and the Europeans, and with the help of the Indians in the North European area. Student writes: "The Indians can help them."

Prior Knowledge. Does the reader's knowledge of the world affect comprehension?

Subj. 002: Student refers to Squanto as a boy from the India[n] race." Perhaps what student knows about Indians and Cowboys from movies or even in his/her readings prompted student to think that the Pilgrims must have been helped by an innocent Indian boy rather than an adult Indian savage. Student also describes Squanto as a "responsible" person because he had taught the Pilgrims how to build shelter for winter.

REFERENCES

Adams, M. J. & Collins, A. 1985. A schema-theoretic view of reading. In H. Singer & R. Press.

Aebersold, J. N. & Field, M. 1. 1997. *From reader to reading teacher: Issues and strategies for second language classrooms.* Cambridge: Cambridge University Press.

Aiken, L. R. 1987. Testing with multiple-choice items. *Journal of Research and Development in Education,* 20, 44-58.

Alderson.J. C. 1980. Native and non-native speaker performance on doze tests. *Language Learning,* 30,597-6.

Alderson, J. C. 1984. Reading in a foreign language: A reading problem or a language problem? In J. C. Alderson & A. H. Urquhart (Eds.), *Reading in a foreign language.* 1-24 London: Longman.

Alderson, J. c. & Urquhart, A. H. 1984. Introduction: What is reading. In J. C. Alderson & A. H. Urquhart (Eds.), *Reading in a foreign language.* xv-xxviii, London: Longman.

Alderson, J. C. & Urquhart, A. H. 1988. This test is unfair: I'm not an economist. In P. L. Carrell, J. Devine & D. E. Eskey (Eds.), *Interactive approaches to second language reading,* 168-182. Cambridge: Cambridge University.

Allen, E. D., Bernhardt, E. B., Berry, M. T. & Demel, M. 1988. Comprehension and text genre: An analysis of secondary school foreign language readers. *Modern Language Journal,* 72(2), 163-172.

Amlund, J. T., Kardash, C. M. & Kulhavy, R. W 1986. Repetitive reading and recall of expository text. *Reading Research Ouarterly,* 21(1), 49-58.

Anderson, R. C. 1985. Role of the reader's schema in comprehension, learning, and memory. In H. Singer & R. B. Ruddell (Eds.), *Theoretical models and processes of reading* (3rd ed.), 372-384. Newark, DL: International Reading Association.

Anderson, R. C. & Pearson, P. D. 1988. A schema-theoretic view of basic processes in reading comprehension. In P. L. Carrell, J. Devine & D. E. Eskey (Eds.), *Interactive approaches to second language reading.* Cambridge: Cambridge University Press.

Anderson, R. C., Reynolds, R. E., Schallert, D. L. & Goetz, T. E. 1977. Frameworks for comprehending discourse. *American Educational Researchjournal, 14,* 367-381.

Anderson, R. c., Spiro, R.J. &Anderson, M. C. 1978. Schemata as scaffolding for the representation of information in connected discourse. *American Educational Research journal,* 15,433-440.

Athey, I. 1985. Language models and reading. In H. Singer & R. Ruddell (Eds.), *Theoretical models and processes of reading* (3rd ed.), 35-62. Newark, DL: InternationalReadingAssociation.

Badger, E. 1990. *Using different spectacles to look at student acbieuement; Implications for theory and practice.* Paper presented at the American Educational Research Association, Boston, MA. (ERIC Document Re- production Service No. ED 320 938).

Bartholomae, D. & Petrosky, A. R. 1986. *Facts, artifacts, and counterfacts.* Upper Montclair, NJ: Boynton/Cook.

Bartlett, F. C. 1932. *Remembering.* New York: Macmillan.

Bender, T. A. 1980. *Processing multiple-choice and recall/est questions.* Paper presented at the American Educational Research Association Annual Meeting, Boston, MA. (ERIC Document Reproduction Service No. ED 189 160).

Berkemeyer, V B. 1989. *Die Unterrichspraxis,* 22, 131-137. Qualitative analysis of immediate recall protocol data: Some classroom implications Bernhardt, E. B. 1983. Three approaches to reading comprehension in intermediate German. *Modern Language journal, 67,* 111-115.

Bernhardt, E. B. 1985. A model of L2 text reconstruction: The recall of literacy text by learners of German. In A. Labarca & 1. M. Bailey (Eds.), *Issues in L2: Theory as practice, practice as theory,* pp. 21-43. NorWOOd, NJ: Ablex.

Bernhardt, E. B. 1986. Reading in a foreign language. In B. H. Wing (Ed.), *Listening, reading, writing: Analysis and application.* 93-115. Middlebury VT: Northeast Conference on the Teaching of Foreign Languages.

Bernhardt, E. B. 1988. *Merging research and assessment: Perspectives in foreign language reading,* Ohio: Ohio State University, Foreign Language Education. Technical report submitted to Institute of Advanced Studies, National Foreign Language Center, Ohio.

Bernhardt, E. B. 1991. *Reading development in a second language: Theoretical, empirical & classroom Perspectives.* Norwood, NJ: Ablex.

Bernhardt, E. B. & Berkemeyer, V B. 1988. Authentic texts and the high school German learner. *Die Unterrichspraxis,* 21(1),6-28.

Bernhardt, E. B. & James, C.J. 1987. *The teaching and testing of comprebension in foreign language learning.* Paper presented at the 1987 Central States Conference. (ERIC Document Reproduction Service No. ED 285 420)

Bloome, D. & Green, J. 1984. Directions in the sociolinguistic study of reading, In P. D. Pearson (Ed.), *Handbook of reading research* (pp. 395-421). New York: Longmans.

Brancard, R. & Hind, J. 1989. *Ready to read.* New York, NY: Oxford University Press.

Bransford, J. D. & Johnson, M. K. 1972. Contextual prerequisites for understanding: Some investigations of comprehension and recall. *Journal of Verbal Learning and Verbal Behavior,* 11,717-726.

Brewer, J. K. 1988. *Introductory statistics for researchers* (4th ed.). Edina, MN: Burgess International Group.

Bridge, C. 1987. Strategies for promoting reader-text interactions. In R.J. Tierney, P. L. Anders & J. N. Mitchell (Eds.), *Understanding readers' understanding: Theory and practice,* 283-305. Hillsdale, NJ: Lawrence Erlbaum.

Brown, H. D. 1987. *Principles of language learning and teaching.* New Jersey: Prentice-Hall.

Brown, J. D. 1988. *Understanding research in second language learning.* New York, NY: Cambridge University Press.

Carrell, P. L. 1983. Three components of background knowledge in reading comprehension. *Language Learning,* 33, 183-207.

Carrell, P. L. 1984a. Evidence of a formal schema in second language comprehension. *Language Learning,* 34, 87-113.

Carrell, P. L. 1984b. The effects of rhetorical organization on ESL readers. *lESOL Quarterly,* 18,441-470.

Carrell, B L. 1988. Introduction: Interactive approaches to second language reading. In P. L. Carrell, L. Devine & D. E. Eskey (Eds.), *Interactive approaches to second language reading.* 1- 7. Cambridge: Cambridge University Press.

Carrell, P .L. & Connor, U. 1991. Reading and writing descriptive and persuasive texts. *Modem Language Journal,* 75, 314-324.

Carrell, P. L., Devine, J. & Eskey, D. E. (Eds.). 1988. *Interactive approaches to second language reading.* Cambridge: Cambridge University Press.

Carrell, P. L. & Eisterhold, J. C. 1988. Schema theory and ESL reading pedagogy. In P L. Carrell, J. Devine & D. E. Eskey (Eds.), *Interactive approaches to second language reading.* Cambridge: Cambridge University Press.

Carrell, P. L. & Floyd, B 1987. Effects on ESL reading of teaching cultural content schemata. *Lanquage Learning,* 37, 89-108.

Carson, J. E., Carrell, P. L., Silberstein, S., Kroll, B. & Kuehn, P. A. 1990. Reading- writing relationships in first and second language. *TESOL Quarterly, 24(2),* 245-266.

Chitravelu, N., Sithampararn, S &The S. C. 1995. *ELTmethodology: Principles and practice.* Shah Alam: Fajar Bakti.

Clark, C. H. 1982. *Assessing free recall. Tbe Readinq Teacher,* 35,434-439. Clarke, M. A. & Silberstein, S. 1977. Toward a realization of psycholinguistic principles in EST reading class. *Language Learning,* 27,135-154.

Coady, J. 1979. A psycholinguistic model-of the ESL reader. In R. Mackay, B. Barkman & R. R. Jordan (Eds.), *Reading in a second language* (pp. 5-12). Rowley, MA: Newbury House.

Collins, A., Brown, J. S. & Larkin, K. M. 1980. Inference in text understanding. In R. J. Spiro, B. C. Bruce & W E Brewer (Eds.), *Theoretical issues in reading comprehension* 385-407. Hillsdale, NJ: Lawrence Erlbaum.

Connor, U. 1984. Recall of text: Differences between first and second language readers. *TESOL Ouarterly,* 18,239-255.

Davey, B. 1989. Assessing comprehension: Selected interaction of task and reader. *The Reading Teacher,* 42, 694-697.

Day, R. R. (Ed.). 1993. *New ways in teaching reading.* Virginia:TESOL.

Demel, M. C. 1990. The relationship between overall reading comprehension of coreferential ties for second language readers of English. *TESOL Quarterly,* 24(2),267-292.

Devine, J. 1988. The relationship between general language competence and second language reading proficiency: Implications for teaching. In P. L. Carrell, J. Devine & D. E. Eskey (Eds.), *Interactiue approaches to second language reading,* 260-277. Cambridge: Cambridge University Press.

Diederich, P. A. 1973. *Short-cut statistics for teacher-made tests.* Princeton, NJ: Educational Testing Service.

Educational Planning and Research Division. 1985. *Education in Malaysia.* Malaysia: Ministry of Education.

Eskey, D. E. 1986. Theoretical foundations. In F. Dubin, D. E. Eskey &W Grabe (Eds.), *Teacbing second language reading for academic purposes 3-23.* Reading, MA: Addison-Wesley.

Eskey, D. E. & Grabe, W 1988. Interactive models for second language readings: Perspective on instruction. In P. L. Carrell, J. Devine & D. E. Eskey (Eds.), *Interactive approaches to second language reading,* 223-238. Cambridge: Cambridge University Press.

Farr, R. & Carey, R. F. 1986. *Reading: What can be measured.?* (2nd ed.). Newark, DE: International Reading Association.

Farr, R., Carey, R. &Tone, B. 1986. Recent theory and research into the reading process: Implications for reading assessment. In J. Orasanu (Ed.), *Reading comprehension: From research to practice,* 135-149. Hillsdale, NJ: Lawrence Erlbaum.

Parr, R., Pritchard, R. & Smitten, B. 1990. A description of what happens when an examinee takes a multiple-choice reading comprehension test. *Journal of Educational Measurement,* 27(3), 209-226.

Frary, R. B. 1985. Multiple-choice versus free-response: A simulation study. *Journal Of Educational Measurement,* 22, 21-30.

Fry, E. 1990. A readability formula for short passages. *Journal Of Reading, 33,* 594-597.

Garcia, G. E. & Pearson, P. D. 1991. *Literacy assessment in a diverse society* (Report No. 525). Urbana, 11: Illinois University, Center for the Study of Reading. (ERIC Document Reproduction Service No. ED 329918)

Goodman, K. S. 1976. Reading: A psycholinguistic guessing game. In H. Singer & R. Ruddell (Eds.), *Theoretical models and processes of reading*. 259-271. Newark, DE: International Reading Association.

Gough, P. B. 1972. One second of reading. In J. F. Kavanaugh & I. C. Maltingly (Eds.), *Language by ear and eye* 331-358. Cambridge, MA: MIT Press.

Grabe, W 1986 The transition from theory to practice in teaching reading. In E Dubin, D. E. Eskey & W Grabe (Eds.), *Teaching second language reading for academic purposes* 25-48. Reading, MA: Addison-Wesley.

Grabe, W 1991. Current developments in second language reading research. *TESOL Quarterly,* 25(3), 375-406.

Grellet, F. 1981. *Developing reading skills: A practical guide to reading comprehension exercises.* Cambridge: Cambridge University Press. Hague, S. A. 1989. Awareness of text structure: The question of transfer from L1 to L2. In S. McCormick & J. Zutell (Eds.), *Thirty-eighth yearbook of the National Reading Conference* 55-64. Rochester, NY: National Reading Conference.

Hague, S. A. 1989. Awareness of text structure: The question of transfer from L1 to L2. In S. McCormick &J. Zutell (Eds.), Thirty-eight yearbook of the National Reading Conference (pp. 55-64). Rochester, NY: National Reading Conference.

Hamrnadou, J. 1988. The effect of analogy on foreign language reading comprehension of advanced and novice readers of French (Doctoral dissertation, Ohio State University, 1988). *Dissertation Abstracts International, 49,*2563.

Harnmadou, J. 1991. Interrelationships among prior knowledge, inference, and language proficiency in foreign language reading. *Modern Language Journal, 75,* 27-38.

Hamsik, M. J. 1984. Reading, readability, and the ESL reader (Doctoral dissertation, Florida State University, 1984). *Dissertation Abstracts International, 45, 2464A.*

Hatch, E. & Lazarathon, A. 1991. *The research manual: Design and statistics for applied linguistics.* New York: Newbury House.

Head, M. H., Readence, J. E. & Buss, R. R. 1989. An examination of summary writing as a measure of reading comprehension. *Reading Research and Instruction, 28(4),* 1-11.

Hudson, T. 1982. The effects of induced schemata on the short "circuit" in L2 reading: Non-decoding factors in L2 reading performance. *Language Learning, 32,* 1-31.

Information Malaysia Yearbook. 1989. Kuala Lumpur, Malaysia: Berita Publishing.

Iran-Nejad, A. C. 1987. The schema: A long-term memory structure or a transient structural phenomena. In R. J. Tierney, P. L. Anders & J. N. Mitchell (Eds.), *Understanding readers' understanding: Theory and practice* 109-127. Hillsdale, NJ: Lawrence Erlbaum.

Irwin, P. A. & Mitchell, J. N. 1983. A procedure for assessing the richness of retellings. *Journal of Reading, 26,* 391-396.

Jenks, F. 1. 1981. Learners' needs and the selection of compatible materials. In J. E. Alatis, H. B. Altman & P. M. Alatis (Eds.), *The second language classroom: Directions for the 1980's* 211- 226. Oxford: Oxford University Press.

Johns, A. M. 1981. Necessary English: A faculty survey. *TESOL Quarterly, 15,* 51-58.

Johnson, T. 1981. Effects on reading comprehension oflanguage complexity and cultural background ofa text. *TESOL Quarterly,* 15(2), 169-181.

Johnson, R. E. 1970. Recall of prose as a function of the structural importance of the linguistic units. *Journal of Verbal Learning and Verbal Behavior, 9,* 12-20.

Johnson, R. E. 1973. Meaningfulness and the recall of textual prose. *American Educational Research journal,* 10,49-58.

Johnston, P. 1984. Prior knowledge and reading comprehension test bias. *Reading Research Quarterly,* 19(2),219-239.

Johnston, P. H. 1983. *Reading comprehension assessment:" A cognitive basis.* Newark, DE: International Reading Association.

Johnston, P. H. 1984. Assessment in reading. In P. D. Pearson (Ed.), *Handbook of reading research* 147-82. New York, NY: Longman.

Johnston, P. H. 1989. Constructive evaluation and the improvement of teaching and learning. *Teachers College Record,* 90, 509-528.

Jorcey, E. 1987. Teaching towards the text and the multiple-choice questions type tests. *System,* 15(1),89-95.

Kamil, M. 1984. Current traditions of reading research. In P. D. Pearson (Ed.), *Handbook of reading research* 39-62. New York, NY: Longman.

Kamil, M. 1986. Reading in the native language. In B. H. Wing (Ed.), *Listening, reading, writing: Analysis and application* 71-91. Middlebury, VT: North- east Conference on the Teaching of Foreign Languages.

Kincade, K. M. 1991. Patterns in children's ability to recall explicit, implicit and metaphorical information. *journal of Research in Reading,* 14(2),81-98.

Kintsch, W & van Dijk, T. A. 1978. Toward a model of text comprehension and production. *Psychological Review,* 85, 363-394.

Kuhn, T. S. 1970. *The structure Of scientific revolutions* (2nd ed.). Chicago: University of Chicago Press.

LaBerge, D. & Samuels, S. 1974. Models of the reading process. In P. D. Pearson (Ed.), *Handbook of reading research,* 185-224. New York, NY: Longman.

Langer, J. A. 1980. Relations between levels of prior knowledge and the organization of recall. In M. L. Kamil & A.J. Moe (Eds.), *Perspectives in reading research and instruction: Twenty-ninth Yearbook of the National Reading Conference* 28-33. Rochester, NY: National Reading Conference.

Langer, J. A. 1987. The construction of meaning and the assessment of comprehension: An analysis of reader performance on standardized items. In R. O. Freedle & R. P. Duran (Eds.), *Cognitive and linguistic analyses of text performance.* 225-244. Norwood, NJ:Ablex.

Langer, J. A. & Nicolich, M. 1981. Prior knowledge and its relationship to com*prehension. Journal of Reading Behavior,* 13(4),373-379.

LaZansky, J., Spencer, F. & Johnston, M. 1987. Reading to learning: Setting students up. In R.J. Tierney, P. L. Anders & J. N. Mitchell (Eds.), *Understanding readers' understanding* 255-281. Hillsdale, NJ: Lawrence Erlbaum.

Lee, J. F. 1986. On the use of the recall task to measure L2 reading comprehension. *Studies* in *Second Language Acquisition,* 8, 83-93.

Lee, J. F. 1990. Constructive processes evidenced by early stage non-native readers of Spanish in comprehending an expository text. *Hispanic Linguistics,* 4(1),129-148.

Lee, J. E, & Musumeci, D. (1988). On hierarchies of reading skills and text types. *Modern Language Journal,* 72(2), 173-187.

Lee, J. F. & Riley, G.L. 1990. The effect of prereading, rhetorically-oriented frameworks on the recall of two structurally different expository texts. *Studies in Second Language Acquisition,* 12,25-41.

Lim, K. B. 1976. Issues in the teaching of English as a second language in Malaysia. In D. Feitelson (EeL), *Mother tongue or second language?: On the teaching of reading in multilingual societies* 21-31. Newark, DE: International Reading Association.

Lutjeharrns, M. (1982, August). *Testing reading comprehension: An example from German for academic purposes.* Paper presented at the International Symposium on Language for Specific Purposes, Eindhoven, Netherlands. (ERIC Document Reproduction Service No. ED 225 347)

Lutjeharrns, M. 1986. The use of L1 in foreign language reading comprehension. In D. Vincent, A. K. Pugh & G. Brooks (Eds.), *Assessing reading 148-162.* Houndmills, UK; Macmillan Education.

Maarof, N. 1993. Assessing reading comprehension of Malaysian ESL university students: A comparison between an immediate written recall task and a multiple-choice task. (Doctoral Dissertation, The Florida State University, 1993). Dissertation Abstracts International, 93)

Mandler, J. M., Scribner, S., Cole, M. & DeForest, M. 1980. Cross-cultural invariance in story recall. *Child Development,* 51,19-26.

Meyer, B.J. E 1975. *The organization of prose and its effects on memory.* Amsterdam: North-Holland.

Meyer, B. F. 1985. Prose analysis: Purposes, procedures, and problems. In B. K. Brittan & J. B. Black (Eds.), *Understanding expository text.· A theoretical and practical handbook for analysing explanatory text* 11-64 Hillsdale, NJ: Lawrence Erlbaum.

Meyer, B. F. & Freedle, R. O. 1984. Effects of discourse type on recall. *American Educational Research journal,* 21 (I), 121-143.

Meyers, S. S. 1991. Performance in reading comprehension product or process? *Educational Review,* 43(3), 257-272.

Norusis, M. N. 1991. *SPSS/PS+ Studentware plus.* Chicago, 11: SPSS Ine. Ostler, S. (1981). A survey of academic needs for advanced ES1. *TESOL Quarterly,* 14,489-502.

Nuttall, C. 1996. *Teaching reading skills in a foreign language.* Oxford: Heinemann.

Oller, J. W Jr. 1979. *Languagetestsatschool:Apragmaticapproach.* London: Longman.

Oosterhof, A. C. 1990. *Classroom applications of educational measurement.* Ohio: Merril.

Pasch, B. 1986. *The readability machine* [Computerprogram]. Inglewood Cliffs, *NJ:* Prentice-Hall Incorporated.

Pearson, P. D. & Valencia, S. 1987. Assessment, accountability, and professional prerogative. In J. E. Readence & R. S. Baldwin (Eds.), *Research in literacy:merging Perspectives: Thirty-sixth yearbook of the National Reading Conference* 3-16. Rochester, NY: National Reading Conference.

Perfetti, C. A. 1985. *ReadingAbility.* New York: Longman.

Perkins, K. 1984. An analysis of four common item types used in testing EFL reading comprehension. *RELCJournal,* 15,29-43.

Perkins, K. & Parish, C. 1988. *What's wrong with reading comprehension tests?* (ERIC Document Reproduction Service No. ED 297 305)

Pollack, M. 1990. *Some issues in free response testing.* (ERIC Document Reproduction Service No. 322 200)

Powell, W. W. 1988. Compensatory processing strategies in second language reading: An investigation of the effect of thematic context on the cloze task performance of ESL students in a university setting. (Doctoral dissertation, Florida State University, 1988). *Dissertation Abstracts International, 88,* 224-65.

Pyrczak, F. 1975. Passage dependence of reading comprehension questions: Examples. *Journal of Reading,* 18,308-311.

Pyrczak, F. & Axelrod, J. 1976. Determining the passage dependence of reading comprehension exercises: A call for relication. *Journal Of Reading, 19,* 279-283.

Royer, K. & Cunningham, D.J. 1981. On the theory and measurement of reading comprehension. *Contemporary Educational Psychology,* 6,187-216.

Rubin, A. & Hansen.J. 1986. Reading and writing: How are the first two 'IR's" related? In J. Orasanu (Ed.), *Reading comprehension: From research to practice,* 163-170. Hillsdale, NJ: Lawrence Eribaum Associate.

Rumelhart, D. 1977. Toward an interactive-model of reading. In S. Dornie (Ed.), *Attention and performance VI,* 64-82. Hillsdale, NJ: Lawrence Erlbaum.

Rumelhart, D. 1980. Schemata: The building blocks of cognition. In R.J. Spiro, B. C. Bertram & W F. Brewer (Eds.), *Theoretical issues in reading comprehension,* 33-58. Hillsdale, NJ: Lawrence EribaumAssociates.

Samson, D. M. M. 1983. Rasch and reading. In Van Weerean, J. (Ed.), *Practice and problems in language testing theory* 35-39. (Report No. 30). Paper presented at the International Language Testing Symposium. (ERIC Document Reproduction Service No. ED 282 415)

Samuels, S.J. & Kamil, M. 1984. Models of the reading process. In P. D. Pearson, R. Barr, M. Kamil & P. Mosenthal (Eds.), *Handbook of reading research,* 185-224. New York: Longman.

Samuels, S.]. & Kamil, M.1. 1988. Models of the reading process. In P. L. Carrell, J. Devine & D. E. Eskey (Eds.), *Interactive approaches to second language reading,* 22-36. Cambridge: Cambridge University Press.

Schank, R. 1984. *The cognitive computer.* Reading, MA: Addison Wesley. Schank, R. c., & Abelson, R. 1977. *Plans scripts, goals and understanding.* Hillsdale, NJ: Lawrence EribaumAssociates.

Schulz, R. A. 1983. From word to meaning: Foreign language reading instruction after the elementary course. *Modern Language Journal,* 67, 127-134.

Seda, 1. 1989, April-May. *Assessment format and comprehension performance.* Paper presented at the annual meeting of the International Reading Association, New Orleans, LA. (ERIC Document Reproduction Service No. ED 310362).

Shohamy, E. (1984). Does the testing method make a difference? The case of reading comprehension. *Language Testing,* 1,147-170.

Smith, F. 1988. *Understanding reading* (4th ed.). Hillsdale, NJ: Lawrence Erlbaum.

Smith, S. P. & Jackson, J. H. 1985. Assessing reading/ learning skills with written retellings. *Journal of Reading,* 28, 622-630.

Spiro, R.J. 1980. Constructive processes in prose comprehension and recall. In R.J. Spiro, B. C. Bruce & W F. Brewer (Eds.), *Theoretical issues in reading comprehension,* 245-278. Hillsdale, NJ: Lawrence Erlbaum.

Spiro, R.J., & Myers, A. 1984. Individual differences and underlying cognitive process in reading. In P. D. Pearson (Ed.), *Handbook Of reading research* 471-501. New York: Longman.

Spivey, N. N. 1989. *Construing constructivism: Reading research in the United* States (Report No. 12). Berkeley: University of California, Center for the study of Writing. (ERIC Document Reproduction Service No. ED 310 358)

Stanovich, K. E. 1980. Toward an interactive-compensatory model of individual differences in the development of reading fluency. *Reading Research Quarterly,* 16, 32-71.

Stathman, S. 1979. Testing reading comprehension: Multiple-choice v. short- answer questions. *English Language Teaching,* 33(4), 304-306.

Statman, S. 1988. Ask a clear question and get a clear answer: An enquiry into the question/answer and sentence completion formats of multiple-choice items. *System,* 16(3),367-376.

Steffensen, M. S., Ioag-dev, c. &Anderson, R. C. 1979. A cross-cultural perspective on reading comprehension. *Reading Research Quarterly,* 15(1), 10-29.

Sternberg, R.J. 1991. Are we reading too much into reading comprehension tests? *Journal of Reading,* *34G), 540-545.*

Stotsky, S. 1983. Research on reading/writing relationships: A synthesis and suggested directions. *Language Arts,* 60, 627 -642.

Tan, S. H. & Ling, C. P. 1979. The performance of a group of Malay-medium students in an English reading comprehension test. *RELCJournal,* 10(1),81-89.

Taylor, B. M. 1980. Children's memory for expository text after reading. *Reading Research Quarterly,* 15,399-411.

Taylor, B. M. 1985. The search for a meaningful approach to assessing comprehension of expository text. In J. A. Niles (Ed.), *Changing perspectives on research in reading/language processing and instruction: Thirty-third yearbook of the National Reading Conference* 257-263. Rochester, NY: National Reading Conference.

Valencia, S. W, Stallman, A. c., Commeyras, M., Pearson, P. D. & Hartman, D. K. 1991. Four measures of topical knowledge: A study of construct validity. *Reading Research Quarterly,* 26(3),204-233.

Von Glasersfeld, E. 1988, July-August. *Environment and Communication.* Paper presented at the ICME-6, Budapest, Hungary. (ERIC Document Reproduction Service No. ED 295 850)

Von Glasersfeld, E. 1989a. *Knowing without metaphysics: Aspects of the radical constructivist position.* (Report No. SRRI-208). Kitchener, Ontario: Kitchener-Waterloo Record. (ERIC Document Reproduction No. ED 304344)

Von Glasersfeld, E. 1989b. *An exposition of constructivism: W'by some like it radical.* (Report No. SRRI-224). Amherst, MA: Massachusetts University, Scientific Reasoning Research Institute. (ERIC Document Reproduction Service No. ED 309 935)

Voss, J. F., Tyler, S. W & Bisanz, G. 1. 1982. Prose comprehension and memory. In C. R. Puff (Ed.), *Handbook of research methods in human memory and cognition* 349-383. New York: Academic Press.

Warren, W H., Nicholas, D. W & Trabasso, T. 1979. Event chains and inferences in understanding narratives. In R. O. Freedle (Ed.), *New directions in discourse processing.* 23-52. Norwood, NJ:Ablex.

Wells, D. R. 1986. The assessment of foreign language reading comprehension: Refining the task. *Die Unterricbspraxis,* 19, 178-184.

Wesdorp, H. (1983, March). Backwash effects of multiplechoice language tests: Myth or reality? In J. Van Weeren (Ed.), *Practice and problems in language testing* 5: *Non-classical test theory final examinations in secondary schools*

(Report No. 30). 79-89. Paper presented at the International Language Testing Symposium, Arnheim, Netherlands. (ERIC Document Reproduction Service No. ED 282 415)

Widdowson, H. G. 1979. *Explorations on applied linguistics.* Oxford: Oxford University Press.

Wilson, P. T. &Anderson, R. C. 1986. What they don't know will hurt them: The role of prior knowledge in comprehension. In J. Orasanu (Ed.), *Reading comprehension: From research to practice,* 31-48. Hillsdale, NJ: Lawrence Erlbaum.

Winograd, P., Paris, S. & Bridge, C. 1991. Improving the assessment of literacy. *The Reading Teacher,* 45(2), 108-116.

Wixson, K. K. & Peters, C. W 1987. Comprehension assessment: Implementing an interactive view of reading. *Educational Psychologist, 22,* 333-356.

Wolf, D. F. 1991. The effects of task, language assessment, and target language experience on foreign language learners performance on reading comprehension tests. *Dissertation Abstracts International, 52,* 832A.

Wolff, D. 1987. Some assumptions about second langauge text comprehension. *Studies in Second Language Acquisition,* 9,307-326.

Yochum, N. 1991. Children's learning from informational text: The relationship between prior knowledge and text structure. *Journal of Reading Behavior,* 23(1),87-103

REFERENCES – ALTERNATIVE ASSESSMENT

References

Barrett, H. (2003). *Electronic portfolio development.* Retrieved June 12, 2006, from http://newali. apple.com/ali_sites/ali/exhibits/1000156/

Costa, A. L., & Kallick, B. (1995). *Assessment in the learning organization: Shifting the paradigm.* Alexandria, VA: Association for Supervision and Curriculum Development.

Donna, J., Cole, C. W. R., Kick, F., & Mathies, B. K. (2000) *Portfolios across the curriculum and beyond.* Thousand Oaks, CA: Corwin Press, Inc.

Elango, S., Jutti, R. C., & Lee, L. K. (2005). *Portfolio as a learning tool: Students' perspective.* Retrieved April 22, 2006, from www.annals.edu.sg/pdf/ 34VolNo8200509/V34N8p511.pdf

Fogarty, R., Burke, K., & Belgrad, S. (1996). The portfolio connection: Real-world examples. In R. Fogarty (Ed.), *Student portfolios: A collection of articles* (pp. 89-100). Illinois: SkyLight Training and Publishing.

Hiang, P. S. (1997). *The evaluation of primary science project using portfolio.* Unpublished master's thesis, Maktab Perguruan Tuanku Bainun, Bukit Mertajam, Pulau Pinang, Malaysia.

Hill, B. C. (2005). *Incorporating student voice: Portfolios and student -led conferences.* Paper presented at the ECIS Conference, Netherlands.

Johnston, P., & Costello, P. (2005). Principles for literacy assessment [Electronic version]. *Reading Research Quarterly, 40*(2), 256–267.

Kemp, J., & Toperoff, D. (1998). *Guidelines for portfolio assessment in teaching English.* Retrieved August 1, 2005, from http://www.anglit.net/main/portfolio/default.html

Klenowski, V. (2002). *Developing portfolios for learning and assessment: Processes and principles.* London: RoutledgeFlammer.

Mabry, L. (1999). *Portfolio plus: A critical guide to alternative assessment.* Thousand Oaks, CA: Corwin Press.

Melograno, V. J. (1996). Portfolio assessment: Documenting authentic student learning. In R. Fogarty (Ed.), *Student portfolios: A collection of articles* (pp. 149-168). Illinois: SkyLight Training and Publishing.

Moersch, C., & Fisher III, L. M. (1996) Electronic portfolios - Some pivotal questions. In R. Fogarty (Ed.), *Student portfolios: A collection of articles* (pp. 111-126). Illinois: SkyLight Training and Publishing.

Mohd Asri Mohd Noor. (n.d.). *Malaysian university students' perception on the use of portfolio as an assessment tool in an ESL writing classroom.* Retrieved June 12, 2005, from http://arc.dg21.com/forms/directory.phpdirectory_id=55

Murphy, S., & Smith, M. A. (1991). *Writing portfolios: A bridge from teaching to assessment.* Ontario, Canada: Pippin Publishing.

Nasirun, J. (n.d.). *Sekolah bestari* [Smart schools]. Retrieved June 12, 2005, from http://members.tripod.com/~Friend4/bestrai.html

Paulson, F. L., & Paulson, P. R. (1996). Assessing portfolios using the constructivist paradigm. In R. Fogarty (Ed.), *Student portfolios: A collection of articles* (pp. 27-46). Illinois: SkyLight Training and Publishing.

Richards, C. (2005). *Activity-reflection e-portfolios: An approach to the problem of effectively integrating ICTs in teaching and learning.* Retrieved August 15, 2005, from http://lsn.curtin.edu.au/tlf/tlf2005/refereed/richards.html

Shaklee, B. D. (1997). *Designing and using portfolios.* Boston, MA: Allyn and Bacon.

Tileston, D. W. (2004). *What every teacher should know about student assessment.* Thousand Oaks, CA: Corwin Press.

Ying, B. P. (2002). *Perlaksanaan kerja kursus berportfolio dalam kursus diploma perguruan Malaysia.* Unpublished doctoral dissertation, University Kebangsaan Malaysia, Selangor. Malaysia.

Printed in the United States
By Bookmasters